CONTENTS

ACKNOWLEDGEMENTS

I want to thank my colleague David Noakes and two of our Issachar Ministries trustees – Vanessa Edmonds and Aggy Efthimiou for their kindness in reading the manuscript of this book and making many helpful corrections and suggestions.

I am most grateful to the Revd Jock Stein for typesetting this book and to John Scriven of Wilberforce Publications for his willingness to publish it, and for the speed with which they have produced it.

I'm particularly grateful to my wife Monica for carrying all the load of the ministry that we usually jointly carry and shielding me from the multitude of emails and other burdens so that I could write this book in just six weeks during the pandemic lockdown.

Other recent books by Dr Hill

Listening with Understanding – Discerning God's Voice, Sovereign World Publishers, Lancaster 2011

Free at Last? – The Tottenham Riots and the Legacy of Slavery, Wilberforce Publications, London 2014

Living in Babylon – A Study of the Sixth Century BC Jewish Exile, Handsel Press, Edinburgh 2016 (jointly with Monica Hill)

The Reshaping of Britain – Church and State since the 1960s: a Personal Reflection, Wilberforce Publications, London 2018

FOREWORD

It is a privilege to write a Foreword to this latest book by my friend and colleague of many years, Clifford Hill.

More than 40 years have passed since I was gripped by reading his book *Towards the Dawn*; and there is now a sense of the wheel having turned full circle as we have watched the scenario anticipated in that book become reality.

Living in these unprecedented times of global turmoil and upheaval, we are seeing in our own lifetime the beginning of the *"birth-pains"* of the times which Jesus predicted to his disciples in the Olivet Discourse (Matt 24:8). We see increasingly the rebellion of the nations against God and his Messiah as predicted in Psalm 2; and the present global coronavirus pandemic, which has come upon us, is a clear warning sign that the time for repentance is running out.

Clifford Hill's sociological expertise, together with his love and knowledge of the Word of God and in particular the writings of the Hebrew prophets, equips him uniquely to understand the significance of the dark days in which we are now living and to see how our nation of Britain has increasingly plumbed the depths of secular humanism and turned away from God who has blessed us in former times and saved us miraculously from certain defeat at the hands of our enemies. The voice of God through the professing Church has been silenced by increasing deception and unbelief, and by the desire to conform to the culture of a society which has turned its back on His ways revealed in the Bible.

The essential and urgent message of this book is a warning that as a nation we are living in days like those of the nation of Judah when God could no longer endure their idolatry, false teaching and false prophecy, and the shedding of the innocent blood of children in the fires of sacrifice to false gods. As Judah was besieged by the armies of Babylon, so we are now besieged by a new and deadly pandemic of sickness and the resulting economic collapse which is staring us in the face.

God has us cornered; after years of warnings to our society which has turned its back upon Him who is both Creator and Sovereign over the world in which we live, we must either repent or face yet worse afflictions. We have brought down on our own heads the consequences of the path we have chosen by rejecting Him. The result of the path we have chosen is that our society is sick in ways which will bring us to destruction unless we humble ourselves and seek the only effective remedy; as God says in Isaiah 45:22, *"Turn to me and be saved, all the ends of the earth, for I am God and there is no other"*.

My prayer is that this book will stir the hearts of all who read it, and that repentance and a sustained outpouring of prayer will result. If we respond, there is yet hope of God's mercy and of a fresh outpouring of his Spirit to equip his people to bring the message of salvation to our stricken nation. The hour is late and the darkness is increasing, but God's desire is still to turn us back from the very brink of disaster where we now stand.

David Noakes

01.08.2020

INTRODUCTION

By the beginning of August 2020 more than 40,000 people had died in the UK from the coronavirus pandemic. The full lockdown of the nation had been eased but restrictions on movement, especially on contact with others outside household or restricted bubbles, were still being enforced. Regional lockdowns were still in place where there were high rates of infection. Places of entertainment and sports arenas had remained closed since March 2020. The nation had borne the full national lockdown restrictions stoically with almost 100% compliance which sparked considerable adverse publicity when a few high-profile individuals broke the regulations.

These individual cases actually highlighted the continuing compliance of the nation in its response to the pandemic and the amazing acts of kindness and self-sacrifice as people sought to help each other, to shield the elderly and vulnerable, and to provide food for the housebound. The NHS staff and ambulance crews had responded magnificently to the needs of the nation which was recognised by people coming out of their houses weekly during the lockdown to clap and publicly give thanks for the selfless ways the health services staff, including care homes staff and carers, were serving during the crisis.

The National Lockdown

Looking back at the national lockdown in the spring and early summer of 2020, for those not living in overcrowded houses, it gave plenty of time for reflection. There was an eerie quietness in the high streets, on the roads and in the air above the nation as 95% of flights were cancelled and public transport and traffic almost came to a standstill. All theatres and most shops and the nation's schools were closed. Even the churches were closed for the first time in history.

When the shutdown began in March no one knew that it was to last for more than three months and then the lockdown was only slowly eased with no formal normality in sight and the Prime Minister saying that he "hoped things would be back to normal by Christmas". Of course, he did not specify which Christmas!

Preparation and Protection

It appears to be a national trait of the British that we are never prepared when major events take place. When Germany and Japan in the 1930s were building vast armies in preparation for war, the British did nothing despite the warnings of Winston Churchill. But once war was forced upon us the British people moved rapidly into top gear, producing everything from Spitfires to the Home Guard.

Similarly, at the beginning of 2020, although there had been talk of a worldwide pandemic for several years, and some countries had made provision, the British had done very little. So, we lacked even the basic Personal Protection Equipment (PPE) required to protect our frontline nurses and doctors on duty in the hospitals. But as always in times of crisis, the British public rose to the need and thousands of recently retired doctors and nurses responded to the call to come back on duty and many more thousands of the public volunteered for a range of duties.

Emergency 'Nightingale' hospitals were built with the aid of the army in a few days as the whole nation adjusted to the demands of the crisis. The nation was shaken when Prime Minister Boris Johnson contracted the virus and was admitted to St Thomas's Hospital in London and was soon taken into intensive care. He was the focus of intense prayer from right across the country as people feared that his death would be a sign of judgment on the nation. Undoubtedly God responded to the prayers of the people and he made a recovery in a remarkably short time.

A Second Plague

The coronavirus pandemic, however, was not the only event hitting the nations in the spring and summer of 2020. A second plague – a plague of locusts – was also afflicting many nations in the Middle East and Africa. It was reported to be the greatest plague of locusts ever seen. It began in a desert area around the Gulf of Oman in 2018, when exceptional storms swept the area generating a voracious breed of desert locusts that swarmed on both sides of the Gulf with Iran on one side and Oman, Yemen and Saudi Arabia on the other side.

The work of controlling the spread of the locusts through insecticides and aerial spraying was hampered by the lockdowns caused by the coronavirus pandemic. The locusts, which can eat as much food in a single day as would be consumed by 35,000 people, were already laying eggs in May 2020 that would hatch and generate the next swarm in July 2020 bringing famine and starvation to millions of people.

It was an extraordinary time for a plague of locusts to hit a large area of the world at the same time as the coronavirus pandemic was hitting nations in every region of the world! So, what was the significance of this phenomenon?

In the Bible God uses plagues to send strong messages to people. He used plagues to force Egypt to let the people of Israel go from slavery, and there are many more examples. Jeremiah says that the sword, famine, and plagues are God's instruments of sending warnings or judgment, and they are usually accompanied by calls for repentance. So how are we to interpret what began happening in December 2019 in Wuhan China and developed into not just one worldwide plague but two, simultaneously hitting the nations?

God's Purpose

Surely God must have some extraordinary purpose in sending, or allowing, TWO plagues at the same time. This is what we want to investigate in this book, and this will be done by looking at the nature and purposes of God and the ways in which he acts as recorded in the Bible.

The prophet Joel used a plague of locusts to warn of an invasion by enemies of Israel who would devastate the land: *"Before them the land is like the garden of Eden, behind them, a desert waste – nothing escapes them"* (Joel 2:3). He used this threat of invasion to call for repentance:

"Rend your heart, and not your garments. Return to the Lord your God, for he is gracious and compassionate, slow to anger and abounding in love, and he relents from sending calamity" (Joel 2:13).

But Joel also foresaw a time coming when God would judge all nations – particularly for what they had done to his covenant people of Israel. This would be the benchmark by which the nations are judged according to Joel. He says:

"In those days and at that time, when I restore the fortunes of Judah and Jerusalem, I will gather all nations and bring them down to the valley of Jehoshaphat. There I will enter into judgment against them concerning my inheritance, my people Israel, for they scattered my people among the nations and divided up my land" (Joel 3:1-2).

It is worth noting at this point, that the nation hardest hit by a combination of both the Covid 19 pandemic and the plague of locusts was Iran, the leading nation in the Middle East calling for the total destruction of Israel.

Unrest

The Covid 19 pandemic was still at its height when widespread public unrest was stirred in a movement that became known as 'Black Lives Matter', caused by the death of a black man who had been arrested by police in Minneapolis USA, with video film of the white policeman kneeling on the man's neck until he died. This sparked worldwide demonstrations which followed a similar pattern to the 'Extinction Rebellion' movement in 2019, the climate change campaign that had gripped the minds and hearts of millions of children in the Western nations. This was largely as an outcome of Greta Thunberg, the Swedish school girl, who had shot to world fame with her demands that the older generation should listen to the young people who will have to live with the consequences of the older generation's reckless disregard of the pollution of the air, the sea and the land.

The largest demonstrations were seen in America where tens of thousands gathered in many cities in total disregard of social distancing. Minneapolis police headquarters were burned to the ground and there was considerable violence in many other cities across the USA that continued for more than a week with demands for the defunding of the police force in a number of cities with serious challenges to law and order. But the ignoring of social distancing in the demonstrations had a serious effect upon the spread of the coronavirus pandemic and the USA rapidly rose to the highest rate of infections in the world.

Searching for Answers

In Britain during the early stages of the national lockdown there were clear signs of an awakening of spiritual interest in many people who were not churchgoers and maybe had never attended churches. They were searching for something beyond the everyday demands of life, and were especially looking for answers to questions about what was going on the world today.

When the churches shut at the beginning of the lockdown, pastors sought ways of communicating with their congregations to offer comfort and spiritual guidance. Preachers were keen to get a message out to any who would listen, and this resulted in the rapid development of different methods, using Zoom and other Internet media, for streaming words and music to any who were able to receive it on their computers or phones.

Research showed that 25% of the population were listening to these messages from religious institutions which showed a hunger in the nation. The weekly online magazine *Prophecy Today UK*[1] of which I have been the editor since 2015 saw a rapid increase in numbers of those who were reading it. Clearly there was a demand among Christians for a Bible-based perspective on the crisis that was surrounding us. The question *"Is there any word from the Lord?"* was on the lips, or in the minds of many Christians.

Silent Church Leaders

Similar questions were at the heart of the search among non-Christians for answers that were beyond human rationality, as to what lay behind the pandemic and the associated upheaval it caused. The silence of church leaders and their failure to respond to the needs of the population left a large gap in the media that was not being filled. The opportunity was there to bring a word from God to a hungry nation.

It seemed incredible that no one among prominent church leaders of any denomination was responding to the needs of the nation. The messages being streamed from most local church leaders were no different from those they would have been giving in their churches under normal circumstances. They did not search the Scriptures for an understanding of the ways of God and what he might be saying to the nations today in the face of these extraordinary circumstances.

---

1 The forerunner was the printed magazine *Prophecy Today* which ran from 1985 to 2005 and had the largest UK circulation of Christian magazines in the 1990s.

They were, in fact, behaving in the same way as the religious leaders in Jerusalem in the time of Jesus when he said to them that they were better at giving a weather forecast than in interpreting spiritual matters to the people. *"You know how to interpret the appearance of the sky, but you cannot interpret the signs of the times"* (Matt 16:3). That same charge could be made against church leaders today.

It was this silence among church leaders today that prompted the writing of this book.

Methodology

It is my profound hope that what is written here may bring some understanding of what is happening today. The methodology followed here is to examine the nature and purposes of God as revealed in the Bible through his covenant activity in the history of Israel and through the revelation of truth given through the biblical prophets. This enables us to perceive the significance of what God is saying and doing in our lifetime.

CHAPTER 1

SHAKING THE NATIONS

Silent Churches

Why were the churches silent in the early months of the coronavirus pandemic? Why were there no statements from church leaders to give guidance to the political leaders of the nation at this critical time in the history of the nation when spiritual leadership was greatly needed? The whole nation was shaken by the rapid turn of events and the uncertainty amongst the political leaders. It was a great opportunity for church leaders to exercise leadership.

In the ministry in which I have been involved since the 1980s I have been warning that there would come a time in the near future when God would shake all the nations – it is clearly there in Scripture for everyone to read. The great shaking prophesied in the Bible is now with us.

Could it be that the silence of church leaders is due to their lack of conviction that God is at work in the times of crisis in which we are living today? Thinking back through my own ministry, I have been aware of so many things where I have seen the hand of God easily recognisable in the rapidly changing events of recent history. So, it seems incredible to me that all church leaders are not eager to declare the word of God for our times.

Recent History

It was back in the early 1980s that I began to be aware that events reported in our daily newspapers were increasingly like things that had been foreseen by the biblical prophets. I had had a great respect for these prophets since my teenage years. I love their forthrightness and their ability to perceive the spiritual significance of events in their own days and to interpret them to others. But God has not changed, he is the same yesterday, today and for ever. If the prophets of Israel had learned to hear from God of what he was doing in their lifetimes, surely it should be possible for us to do the same today, because God is unchanging – what he said yesterday is true today and forever.

We were clearly living in momentous times of social change and I wanted to meet other Christians who were similarly seeking to explore the possibility that God was directing the changes in our society. Alternatively, were we simply seeing the outworking of the Marxist/Darwinian forces of social change with which I, as a sociologist, was very familiar and which was part of the curriculum my students studied for the London BSc in Sociology earlier in my life.

Need for a Plumb Line of Truth

Even in the early 1980s there was an increase in deception which rapidly increased with the invention of the worldwide web and the spread of fake news, scams and deliberate lies that have become a feature of daily life today. Social media has done much to facilitate the undermining of truth. Deception is so widespread that truth appears to be redefined by those who wish to pursue any deviant political or cultural objectives. But the word of God as declared in the Bible which is the plumb line of truth is rarely heard in the public square and is almost non-existent in our Parliament, or in the news media that focuses upon the trivial statements of so-called 'celebrities'.

The word of God is unchanging, in the same way as God is the unchanging God of yesterday and today. Surely, his truth needs to be heard in the midst of the great shaking of the nations that is happening today. It is this opportunity for discovering the heart of God through what he is doing today that is desperately needed to be communicated to leaders in the nations.

Carmel Gathering

It was in response to my own search for truth that in the early 1980s I began communicating with other church leaders and biblical teachers, not only in Britain, but with any whom I could contact around the world. From this, a small group of seven was formed to organise a larger gathering of those who were exercising similar ministries in different parts of the world. This resulted in a group of 153 meeting at a centre near the summit of Mount Carmel in northern Israel in the spring of 1986. Half of them were leaders of churches or of parachurch organisations exercising ministry. Each of them, because of the differences in culture and language in such an international group, was invited to bring with them a trusted intercessor who could pray with them and seek to help in fulfilling the aim of the gathering which was to seek an understanding of what was happening in the world today from a biblical perspective.

Without any publicity, word about the Carmel gathering cascaded rapidly around the world bringing with it a widely expressed desire to be part of such an enquiry. This resulted in a second meeting being organised for the following week in Jerusalem which was attended by 5000 people from many different countries all gathering in the Binyenei Ha'Uma, the Israeli National Conference Centre in Jerusalem.

Both meetings were highly significant, for their timing and their outcome. The Carmel gathering was to meet for seven days of prayer, study and sharing with each other in the search for an understanding of what God is doing and saying to his people today. The second gathering was for worship and study, for hearing what God was saying to the group of leaders at Carmel.

This is not the place to recount in any detail what happened at those two gatherings, but it is right to record that it was the unanimous conviction of all those present that God was warning of the time in the near future when he was going to shake everything – both in the natural environment and in the socio-political affairs of the nations.[2]

It was prophesied at the Jerusalem meeting that the Soviet Union would be the first nation to be shaken. Just three weeks later the Chernobyl nuclear power station disaster occurred which led directly to the ultimate demise of the USSR which until that time, appeared to be an unassailable world power.

---

2 A full report of the events at Carmel and Jerusalem was given in the May/June 1986 issue of the printed magazine *Prophecy Today*, published in London, available through Prophecy Today UK on line.

The Message of Haggai

The two passages in the Bible that most clearly represented what God was saying to us were **Haggai 2:6-7**, and **Hebrews 12:26f**. Both of these Scriptures speak about God shaking everything – the natural environment and the nations. The two prophecies are linked, although they were given with a gap of 500 years between them.

The word in Haggai says: *"**This is what the Lord Almighty says: 'In a little while I will once more shake the heavens and the earth, the sea and the dry land. I will shake all nations, and the desired of all nations will come, and I will fill this house with glory, says the Lord Almighty'.**"*

The word in Hebrews says: *"At that time his voice shook the earth, but now he has promised, once more I will shake not only the earth but also the heavens. The words 'once more' indicate the removing of what can be shaken – that is, created things – so that what cannot be shaken may remain. Therefore, since we are receiving a kingdom that cannot be shaken, let us be thankful, and so worship God acceptably with reverence and awe, for our God is a consuming fire."*

To understand the message being conveyed in each of these passages of Scripture it is necessary to look at the context which is as important as the text if we are rightly to understand its message.

Living in Babylon

Haggai was almost certainly born in Babylon and was among the returning exiles released by Cyrus the Persian when he conquered Babylon in 538 BC. This prophecy was given in Jerusalem eighteen years later – 520 BC in the reign of Darius the King of Persia who had come to the throne just two years earlier.

The company of exiles who returned to Jerusalem were those who had been refined by the experience of living in Babylon, that was a renowned centre of idolatry as well as a great city of commerce. The exiles undoubtedly benefited from the latter and returned with immense riches as recounted in the book of Ezra chapter 2 where they gave a free will offering for a fund to start the rebuilding of the temple amounting to about 500 kg of gold and nearly 3 tons of silver.

The renowned idolatry of Babylon also affected the exiles, but with the reverse effect – generating a hatred of idolatry and a hunger to explore the roots of their own faith. Ezekiel, the prophet of the early days of the exile, was very largely responsible for steering the people away from idolatry and for teaching them the history of Israel and the faith of their fathers, the children of Abraham, Isaac and Jacob.

Ezekiel had been born into one of the aristocratic priestly families ministering in the temple at Jerusalem. He was about 23 years old when he was captured by the Babylonians and taken into exile where, in his fifth year in Babylon, he experienced what he describes as a revelation from God calling him to exercise a prophetic ministry among the scattered communities of Hebrew people in exile.

Teaching the Torah

Ezekiel began a practice of teaching the elders from the different village settlements who came to his house and sat at his feet on a regular basis. They continually asked him if he had any word from the Lord and it was during these times that he expounded the Torah, emphasising the commandments and the need to guard against idolatry as well as the need to pass on the teaching to their children. Ezekiel was an accomplished musician who played an instrument and had a good singing voice (Ez 33.32). From his background as a priest he would undoubtedly have sung the Psalms to the elders and to his own house group and led the men in worship and prayer.

The elders would have taken all these things back to their villages where they would have taught the people and urged them to teach their children and to have regular worship and prayer in the home. In each of the villages there would have been a community meeting place where the heads of families regularly met with the elders.

Synagogues

The meeting place, or 'Knesset', later became known by its Greek name, 'Synagogue'. In the early days of the exile the village Knesset would have been a place of education as well as community meetings, providing instruction in the Torah to boys over the age of 10. The girls would continue their education in the home under the guidance of their mothers. It was in this way that the faith of Judaism was preserved, and the Synagogue became an increasingly important place in the life of the communities. The 'Great Synagogue', or 'Great Assembly' in Babylon became a renowned place of study of the Scriptures, where scrolls of the history of Israel, the five books of Moses and the scrolls of the prophets would all have been studied and copied by the scribes.

Haggai most likely would have sat at the feet of Ezekiel in Babylon and he would also have heard the inspirational words of Isaiah[3] declaring that Babylon would soon be overthrown and God would raise up Cyrus to set the people free to return to the land of their fathers and rebuild Jerusalem. He would have heard such declarations as:

"This is what the Lord says – your Redeemer, who formed you in the womb: I am the Lord, who has made all things, who alone stretched out the heavens, who spread out the earth by myself, who foils the signs of false prophets and makes fools of diviners, who overthrows the learning of the wise and turns it into nonsense, who carries out the words of his servants and fulfils the predictions of his messengers, who says of Jerusalem, it shall be inhabited, of the towns of Judah, they shall be built, and of their ruins, I will restore them, who says of the watery deep, 'Be dry, and I will dry up your streams', who says of Cyrus, he is my Shepherd and will accomplish all that I please; he will say of Jerusalem, let it be rebuilt, and of the temple, let its foundations be laid" (Is 44:24-28).

---

3 All biblical scholars agree that the book of Isaiah is complex and its contents refer to a long period in the history of Israel spanning the eighth century BC to the end of the fifth century and possibly into the fourth century BC. Whether it was all written by one man, excluding chapters 36 to 39 which come from the books of Kings and Chronicles, or whether they are from the hand of several writers in different periods, but all in the Isaiah tradition, is still debated among biblical scholars. In any case, all agree that there is only one author and that is God. I have written at length on these issues elsewhere in my three volumes of *Today with Isaiah* available from Issachar Ministries.

Post-Exilic

It is this prophecy that the temple would be rebuilt that inspired Haggai and caused him to be impatient to see the work of restoration begin. Returning to the ruins of Jerusalem was a devastating experience for the exiles whose first task was to build their own houses to provide shelter for their families. But this did not please Haggai who said that the returning exiles had got their values all wrong. They should put the work on the Lord's house as a priority. This was said in the year 520 BC, some 15 years after the end of the exile and the return of the first wave of people from Babylon.

Re-establishing the shattered economy as well as physically rebuilding the city was an immense task, but Haggai was relentless. When things did not go well in the restoration work and harvests produced insufficient food to sustain the community, he seized his opportunity of berating them. *"Is it a time for you yourselves to be living in your panelled houses, while this house remains a ruin?"* he said.

Haggai's next words give an insight into the social and economic conditions in Jerusalem in the early days of the return from exile. He said: *"Now this is what the Lord Almighty says: 'Give careful thought to your ways. You have planted much but have harvested little. You eat, but never have enough. You drink but never have your fill. You put on clothes but are not warm. You earn wages, only to put them in a purse with holes in it'."*

Haggai did not leave it there: he pressed home his wish to see the temple rebuilt. *"Give careful thought to your ways,"* he said. *"Go up into the mountains and bring down timber and build the house, so that I may take pleasure in it and be honoured, says the Lord."*

Haggai believed in the absolute sovereignty of God, the God of Israel, who was the Creator of the universe. So, he was able to declare that all the hardships and difficulties that the former exiles were experiencing were the direct action of God. He said:

"Therefore, because of you the heavens have withheld their dew and the earth's crops. I called for a drought on the fields and the mountains, on the grain, the new wine, the oil and whatever the ground produces, on men and cattle, and on the labour of your hands," said the Lord (Hag 1:4-11).

The New Temple

Haggai's objective was to get God back into the centre of the life of the community in Jerusalem and to restore faith in the whole nation of Judah – among those who had stayed in the land and those who had returned from Babylon. He saw the rebuilding of the temple as more than just a symbolic act: he wanted to see the whole nation cleansed and renewed, defined by a new holiness and commitment to God.

Haggai may have heard Isaiah's declaration that it was God's purpose to restore the tribes of Jacob and to bring back the tribes of Israel which was also the vision of Jeremiah. But Isaiah in Babylon had said,

"It is too small a thing for you to be my servant to restore the tribes of Jacob and to bring back those of Israel I have kept. I will also make you a light for the Gentiles, that you may bring my salvation to the ends of the earth" (Is 49:6).

This missionary directive was new to the people of Judah, but it helped to fuel the widespread view that the rebuilding of Jerusalem and the temple would be a prelude ushering in the Messianic Age when God would restore the glory of Jerusalem and nations would come to hear the word of God go out from the holy city.

The Message of Hebrews

Hebrews was one of the last books to be written in the New Testament, towards the end of the first century AD, when sporadic opposition to the gospel was breaking out in different parts of the Roman Empire. The writer of Hebrews was intent on building up the faith of Christians to withstand the hardships that they were experiencing. He urged them to see hardship as part of God's discipline to bring out the best in their characters. The whole of chapter 11 is given to recounting the great faith that motivated and strengthened men and women in the past. He concluded the chapter by saying *"These were all commended for their faith, yet none of them received what had been promised. God had planned something better for us so that only together with us would they be made perfect"* (Heb 11:39-40).

The 'something better' that God was planning was none other than the kingdom of God on earth: the 'Messianic Kingdom' that would be established by Jesus at his second coming. By way of introduction, the unknown writer of Hebrews refers to the giving of the first covenant through Moses when the whole house of Israel was gathered at the foot of the mountain, at the 'great assembly' (Exodus 19:17-18) when Moses presented the Decalogue and affirmed the covenant relationship that existed between God and the people of Israel.

Messianic Hope

At that time, the whole mountain was said to be covered in smoke and it shook. The people were terrified, and they were warned not to touch the mountain. But, by contrast, the believers in Jesus had *"come to Mount Zion, to the heavenly Jerusalem, the city of the living God"* (Heb 12:22), where they were part of a 'joyful assembly' initiated by Jesus the 'mediator of a new covenant' who was now promising *"not only to shake the earth but also the heavens"*.

This was part of the messianic hope of the Jewish people that had been with them since the return of the exiles to the land of Judah and the rebuilding of Jerusalem. That hope, which had been born in Babylon, was the strong incentive behind the return. It was connected with the hope for freedom from oppression and from their political overlords in the Persian Empire. That hope for freedom became the new nationalism that outlasted the Persian Empire and the Greek Empire. It was still strong in the days of the Roman Empire at the time of Jesus' ministry. It was connected with every outbreak of violent revolt from the time of the Maccabees to the time of Bar Kokhba in AD 130.

There was a strong political element mixed in with their spiritual aspirations in the popular messianic hope among the people in the time of Jesus. This is seen in the testimonies of those who like Simeon were *"waiting for the consolation of Israel"* (Luke 2:25) and Zechariah whose expectation was that Messiah would *"rescue us from the hand of our enemies, and enable us to serve God without fear in holiness and righteousness before him all our days"* (Luke 1:74).

This political element in the messianic hope was also seen in the desire of the crowds to crown Jesus as King as well as in the hope of zealots such as Judas. It was certainly there in the outbreak of the Jewish War in AD 66 and it was still there in the second century AD until it was finally crushed at the end of the Bar Kokhba revolt in AD 135 when the Jews were finally banished from Judaea, and Jerusalem was renamed Aelia Capitolina by the Emperor Hadrian.

By contrast, the political element had disappeared in the concept presented in Hebrews whose eschatology was now completely centred upon the establishment of the messianic kingdom, which would be purely an act of God. What is envisaged in Hebrews 12 is that God would do something that would shake the whole of creation, both on earth and in the universe.

Shaking the Foundations

The particular objective would be to shake the foundations of human civilisation in order to remove all those parts of the social order that had been created by human beings that were directly against God's teaching. The great shaking would bring about a distinction between humanist institutions that were created in defiance of godly values and the values of the kingdom. This calls for joyful thanksgiving among the believers who form the community of the redeemed – the true *ecclesia* of God.

This kingdom was foreseen by Mary as she looked forward to the birth of Jesus: *"He has scattered those who are proud in their inmost thoughts. He has brought down rulers from their thrones but has lifted up the humble. He has filled the hungry with good things but has sent the rich away empty"* (Luke 1:51-53). It was similarly foreseen by Zechariah, the father of John the Baptist whose mission was to *"prepare the way for the Lord, and give his people the knowledge of salvation through the forgiveness of sins"* and the *splanchna eleous theou hēmōn* – *"the tender depths of compassion of our God"* (Luke 1.77).

It is important to note the difference between what was envisaged by Haggai and by the writer of Hebrews. Haggai's thoughts were centred upon the temple which will be filled with the glory of God. In Hebrews, the concept was not upon a building constructed by human hands but upon a kingdom established by God. As Jesus said to Pilate *"My kingdom is not of this world"*. He said that his kingdom was from *"another place"* and he had come to *"testify to the truth"* (John 18:36-37). The nature of the kingdom was changing from a more material concept to ethereal, from worldly to otherworldly.

The Kingdom of God

The nature of the kingdom of God in the teaching of Jesus is far too complex to summarise in a few sentences, but it undoubtedly turned upside down the values of the world. In the Early Church there was an expectation of the imminent return of Jesus in fulfilment of his own promise that he would come again. This inevitably coloured the expectations of the kingdom, but what did not change was the expectation that at some point in the history of the world God would intervene and shake the whole world of natural creation and all the institutions of human civilisation.

This expectation of divine activity is not dependent upon just the two passages of Scripture that we have examined. There are numerous other references in the Bible, in both Old and New Testaments, to support such a belief. They are scattered among the prophets of Israel and in the teaching of Jesus as well as in the writings of the Apostles.

Isaiah 2 is one of the earliest, dating back to the eighth century BC where the prophet foresees a day coming when God would deal with the pride and arrogance of humanity. He says:

"The Lord Almighty has a day in store for all the proud and lofty, for all that is exalted, and they will be humbled . . . The arrogance of man will be brought low and the pride of men humbled; the Lord alone will be exalted in that day and the idols will totally disappear" (Is 2:12-18).

The Sovereignty of God

Isaiah sees this as a definite act of God *"when he rises to shake the earth"* (Is 2:19). This is fully in line with the later teaching in Isaiah 45:7 where God declares,

*"I form the light and create darkness, **I bring prosperity and create disaster**; I, the Lord, do all these things."*

This is a statement of great significance for an understanding of the sovereignty of God in the teaching of the biblical prophets. The same concept is to be found in Psalms, such as *"Come and see the works of the Lord, **the desolations he has brought on the earth.**"* But this is tempered by the next statement, *"He makes wars cease to the ends of the earth; he breaks the bow and shatters the spear, he burns the shields with fire"* (Ps 46:8-9). Most people like the last part of this statement, but they skip over the desolations – in the same way as we like to talk about the love of God, but we don't talk about his justice.

In this view, God is active in the world in all the affairs and activities of humankind. This, of course, does not mean that God is responsible for all the actions of humanity, but it does mean that he has an overview and is watching over the nations to ensure that his ultimate purposes are achieved and are not thwarted by the sinful actions of human beings.

CHAPTER 2

THE NATURE AND PURPOSES OF GOD

If we are to gain an understanding of what is happening in the world today and why we are seeing plagues and famines and major disturbances in the seasons, and unrest in the nations, we have to study the nature and purposes of God as revealed in the Bible. For this there is a rich tapestry in the history of God's dealings with the people of Israel and with his revelations given to the biblical prophets.

The reason God chose Abraham, his family, and descendants, was not an arbitrary act of favouritism. But it was to be the means for revealing his nature, purposes, and truth to humanity. In the fullness of time he completed that revelation through his Only Begotten Son who was co-existent with the Father – Jesus – who was able to say *"I am the way, the truth, and the life"* as the full and final revelation of God.

A God of Covenant

Moses was told the reason why God had chosen the people of Israel, in a profound statement recorded in Deuteronomy 7:7-10.

"The Lord did not set his affection on you and choose you because you were more numerous than other peoples, for you were the fewest of all peoples. But it was because the Lord loved you and kept the oath he swore to your forefathers that he brought you out with a mighty hand and redeemed you from the land of slavery, from the power of Pharaoh king of Egypt. Know therefore that the Lord your God is God; he is the faithful God, keeping his covenant of love to a thousand generations of those who love him and keep his commands. But those who hate him he will repay to their face by destruction; he will not be slow to repay to their face those who hate him".

This refers to the covenant God made with Abraham after he had responded to the call to leave his country and his people and his father's household to go to the land that God would show him. In response to his obedience and the trust that Abraham had placed in God, he received a promise:

"I will make you into a great nation and I will bless you; I will make your name great, and you will be a blessing. I will bless those who bless you, and whoever curses you I will curse; and all peoples on earth will be blessed through you" (Gen 12:2-3).

This promise was in line with God's creation purposes. It is an expression of his commitment to the marriage-based family that is part of his act of creation, making both man and woman in his own image, capable of communion with him. This is not simply an ideal, it is the only pattern of family that is acceptable in the eyes of God. All deliberate deviations from the faithful, loving, covenant-keeping marriage-based family are unacceptable to God. It is this type of family unit that God has intended from the time of creation to be the means of the procreation of humanity, for the health, welfare and protection of adults, and for the secure and loving raising of children.

The Family of Abraham

To work out his purpose of revealing himself – his nature and purposes to humanity, God chose a family. It was a family headed by a man who had an extraordinary level of faith in God. *"Abraham believed the Lord and he credited it to him as righteousness"* (Gen 15:6). He was a man who was ready to trust God in all circumstances, even when it came to the life of his only son, who was the fulfilment of a promise.

God made a covenant with Abraham of great consequence, beginning with the promise *"You will be the father of many nations. No longer will you be called Abram; your name will be Abraham, for I have made you a father of many nations."* This led to the covenant promise:

"I will establish my covenant as an everlasting covenant between me and you and your descendants after you for the generations to come, to be your God and the God of your descendants after you. The whole land of Canaan, where you are now an alien, I will give as an everlasting possession to you and your descendants after you; and I will be their God" (Gen 17:7-8).

That covenant was confirmed centuries later with the descendants of Abraham following their release from slavery in Egypt. They were a disorganised group of men, women and children and their animals at the beginning of their 40 year trek through the wilderness prior to entering the promised land. It was essential that there should be cohesion and unity among them if they were to survive.

The task of bringing them together as one family under God was given to Moses who several times nearly despaired of them especially when God said he was determined to destroy them for their wilful disobedience and idolatry even by creating a golden calf while Moses was up the mountain and saying that this was the god who had brought them out of Egypt (Ex 32:4). It was only the urgent intercessions of Moses that saved the people from being wiped off the face of the earth. *"Then the Lord relented and did not bring on his people the disaster he had threatened"* (Ex 32:14). Nevertheless, it is recorded that, *"the Lord struck the people with a plague because of what they did with the calf Aaron had made"* (Ex 32:35).

Covenant with Israel

The historic occasion establishing the covenant relationship with the nation of Israel took place at the base of Mount Sinai after Moses had received the Decalogue and called a 'great assembly' of all the people where God said to them:

"Now if you obey me fully and keep my covenant, then out of all nations you will be my treasured possession. Although the whole earth is mine, you will be for me a kingdom of priests and a holy nation." In response all the people said, *"We will do everything the Lord has said."* (Ex 19:5-8).

This covenant relationship with God in which he promised to be their God and they promised that they would be his people was the central plank in the history of Israel from that day. It was referred to many times, usually in times of crisis when things were going wrong in the nation and the people called upon God for help. Moses had clearly set out before the people the need for absolute obedience to the command to have no other God and to obey the teaching that he was given by God. The blessings for obedience and the curses for disobedience are clearly set out in Deuteronomy 28 where it is stated:

"If you do not carefully follow all the words of this law, which are written in this book, and do not revere this glorious and awesome name – the Lord your God – the Lord will send fearful plagues on you

and your descendants, harsh and prolonged disasters and severe and lingering illnesses" (Deut 28:58-59).

In a 'solemn assembly' near the end of his life, Moses summoned all the people together to give them final instructions before they entered the land of Canaan. He was clearly worried at the lack of spiritual discernment among the people. He said that they had all seen what God had done in Egypt, and the miraculous signs and wonders that God had done in bringing them through the desert. But, *"To this day the Lord has not given you a mind that understands or eyes that see or ears that hear"* (Deut 29:4). He was afraid that people would misunderstand the covenant relationship with God and say *"I will be safe, even though I persist in going my own way"*; but Moses warned that this would bring disaster upon the land (Deut 29:19).

Later, in the history of Israel, the fear that Moses had foreseen that the people would misunderstand the covenant relationship with God became a reality in the time of Jeremiah. It was the false religious teaching given by the priests in the temple of which Jeremiah condemned in his 'Temple Sermon' when he warned the people not to believe the teaching of the priests: *"Do not trust in deceptive words and say, 'This is the temple of the Lord, the temple of the Lord, the temple of the Lord!'"* (Jer 7:4).

Moses impressed upon the people the necessity of honouring the terms of the covenant.

"You are standing here in order to enter into a covenant with the Lord your God, a covenant the Lord is making with you this day and sealing with an oath, to confirm you this day as his people, that he may be your God as he promised you and as he swore to your fathers, Abraham, Isaac and Jacob." (Deut 29:12-13).

Moses' final words of warning were:

"Now what I'm commanding you today is not too difficult for you or beyond your reach . . . The word is very near you; it is in your mouth and in your heart so that you may obey it. See, I set before you today life and prosperity, death and destruction. For I command you today to love the Lord your God, to walk in his ways, and to keep his commands, decrees and laws; then you will live and increase, and the Lord your God will bless you in the land you are entering to possess" (Deut 30:11-16).

The Amorites

Moses knew some of the people now occupying the land of Canaan who had originally come from Babylon. They were the Amorites whose sexual practices and idolatry were said to be detestable to God. Moses' great fear was that the people he had led these past 40 years would succumb to the attraction of these people and become involved in their detestable practices. This is what lay behind the strong warnings that he gave to them. His forefathers had been told that at the time when the people of Israel returned to the land *"the sins of the Amorites"* would be full.

The history of the people descended from Abraham was passed down from generation to generation through the families, and it was known that God had said, ***"In the fourth generation your descendants will come back here, for the sin of the Amorites has not yet reached its full measure"*** (Gen 15:16). This is an important statement giving an understanding of God's attitude to certain kinds of sin.

The Amorites were notorious for their mixture of violence and sexual aberrations that included homosexuality and bestiality linked to their idolatry. They worshipped violent sex and lust, turning upside down God's purpose for human reproduction within the marriage-based family. They even included the shedding of innocent blood in their worship by sacrificing infants on the fires of their altars. These were practices that God said were detestable, and as part of the promise to Abraham that at some date in the future his descendants would come back to the land of Canaan, God had said that the sins of the Amorites were not yet full. The implication was that when they reached a certain level, God would no longer withhold judgment.

Soon after Moses was given the commandments at Sinai, God said that when they reached the land of Canaan, he would use Israel to carry out his purpose, to wipe out the Amorites whose detestable practices defiled the land. *"Do not bow down before their gods or worship them or follow their practices. You must demolish them and break their sacred stones to pieces. Worship the Lord your God, and his blessing will be upon your food and water."* (Ex 23:24-25).

This promise of blessing on their food production was particularly necessary because after 400 years of slavery and 40 years as itinerant tribes wandering through wilderness areas with their animals, they had few agricultural skills. They would be dependent upon the local people to impart even basic knowledge to feed their families.

This dependence upon the Canaanites was illustrated in the statement, *"Not a blacksmith could be found in the whole land of Israel, because the Philistines had said, 'Otherwise the Hebrews will make swords or spears!' So all Israel went down to the Philistines to have their ploughshares, mattocks, axes and sickles sharpened"* (1 Sam 13:19-20).

We will take a further look at the Amorites in Chapter 9.

Idolatry and Syncretism

In fact, the Israelites never did drive out the local people to clear the land of idolatry. Inevitably, in times of drought and poor harvests when the tribes of Israel were finding it hard to survive, they listened to their mentors among the Canaanite people who told them that they needed to placate the local gods upon whose land they had settled.

The practices of paying homage to the local Baals on the high places scattered around Israel began very soon after the settlement in the land. It became a permanent feature, mixing the worship of Yahweh with their offerings to the local gods, to the despair of prophets such as Jeremiah, who complained,

"This is what the Lord says: what faults did your fathers find in me, that they strayed so far from me? They followed worthless idols and became worthless themselves. They did not ask, 'Where is the Lord, who brought us up out of Egypt and led us through the barren wilderness?'… I brought you into a fertile land to eat its fruit and rich produce. But you came and defiled my land and made my inheritance detestable" (Jer 2:5-6).

This was the social and spiritual environment that the young king Josiah, at the age of eight, inherited from his grandfather Manasseh following the untimely assassination of his father Ammon. He was about the same age as Jeremiah who warmly approved when the young king, now in his early 20s, instituted a reform programme to purify the land. Five years later he began repairs on the temple that led to the discovery of the 'Book of the Law' and to the renewal of the covenant with God, that was strongly supported by Jeremiah who said *"cursed is the man who does not obey the terms of this covenant"* (Jer 11:3).

Jeremiah's Ministry

Despite coming from a priestly family, Jeremiah did not temper his judgment of responsibility for the spiritual state of the nation, which he saw rested firmly in the hands of the religious leaders of the nation – the priests and prophets. He said,

"From the least to the greatest, all are greedy for gain; prophets and priests alike all practice deceit. They dress the wound of my people as though it were not serious. Peace, peace, they say when there is no peace. Are they ashamed of their loathsome conduct? No, they have no shame at all; they do not even know how to blush" (Jer 6:13-15).

Jeremiah could understand the ordinary people not being aware that their religious practices were offensive to God. They could see no harm in joining with the local Canaanite people in paying respect to their gods at countryside shrines. They went up to Jerusalem for the festivals and paid respect to the God of their ancestors, so they considered they were doing rightly. They also could see no harm in cheating people in their business practices or the produce they sold from their farms.

Jeremiah was told to go up and down the streets of Jerusalem and search for people who dealt honestly and spoke the truth. Finding none he thought *"These are only the poor; they are foolish, for they know not the way of the Lord, the requirements of their God"* (Jer 5:4). So, he went to the leaders but discovered that they also had no regard for the word of the Lord, no commitment to observing the terms of the covenant relationship with God. He was dismayed to observe that *"among the prophets of Jerusalem I have seen something horrible; they commit adultery and live a lie"* (Jer 23:14).

The consequence of their adulterous lifestyles was that they set an example for the people, so that in fact *"They strengthen the hands of evildoers, so that no one turns from his wickedness"* (Jer 23:14). And of even greater consequence for the health and security of the nation was that the religious leaders of the nation were actually telling lies to the people. *"They have lied about the Lord; they said, 'He will do nothing! No harm will come to us; we will never see sword or famine"* (Jer 5:12). They thought that God would always defend the city of Jerusalem and no foreigner could ever enter the temple because God would strike them down, and this is what they taught the people.

Jeremiah knew that this erroneous teaching put the whole nation in danger. The priests and prophets, whose responsibility was to declare the word of God to the nation, did not understand the terms of the covenant between God and the people of Israel. Therefore, they did not know the requirements of God. They did not understand the nature of God – that he is not only a God of love and mercy, who loves his people and is faithful to keep his promises, but he is also a God of justice and righteousness who says that it is righteousness that exalts a nation and sin is a disgrace.

It was the false theology of the religious leaders of the nation, their failure to understand the nature and purposes of God that threatened the lives of everyone in Jerusalem and in the nation of Judah. It was the recognition of this reality that was the huge burden that Jeremiah carried, when he alone among leaders was aware of the vast tragedy that faced them – which never would have happened if there had been repentance and turning in the nation, with people putting their trust in God.

Britain Today

In Britain today, we face a similar situation where the religious leaders of the nation do not know the requirements of God. Senior church leaders are silent in these times of crisis when the nation is searching for an understanding of what is happening in the world, where there is so much confusion and fear and death. The reasons for this we will examine later, but the parallel with the times of Jeremiah needs to be noted.

The most persistent word from God that Jeremiah received throughout his ministry was that neither the leaders nor the people would listen to the warnings that he sent. One message that summarises this is found in Jeremiah 7 from verse 25:

"From the time your forefathers left Egypt until now, day after day, again and again I sent you my servants the prophets. But they did not listen to me or pay attention. They were stiff-necked and did more evil than their fore-fathers . . . This is the nation that has not obeyed the Lord its God or responded to correction. Truth has perished; it has vanished from their lips."

This blindness to the warning signs that God had sent and the words of those with prophetic insight remained throughout the 10 years leading up to the destruction of Jerusalem in 586 BC. It was the obstinacy and deceptive teaching of the leaders that brought tragedy upon the nation.

CHAPTER 3

JUSTICE IN THE NATURE OF GOD

Justice is a central theme running right through the Bible including the teaching of Jesus in the Gospels and Paul in Galatians and Romans. But the Hebraic understanding of justice has been grossly misunderstood in Western theology due to linguistic and etymological differences that have become embedded in Western culture.

In this chapter we are going to attempt to unravel some of these differences which have a bearing upon the activity of God in what we are witnessing today. Until we can understand the justice of God that is part of his nature, we will not be able to understand how God is working out his purposes today. This is why it is essential to study what the Bible teaches us about God's justice.

The Centrality of Justice

Justice is central to the nature of God in the teaching of Moses,

"I will proclaim the name of the Lord. Oh, praise the greatness of our God! He is the Rock. His words are perfect, and all his ways are just. A faithful God who does no wrong, upright and just is he" (Deut 32:3-4).

This statement in the 'Song of Moses' sets out the understanding of God that runs right through the teaching of the prophets and is borne out in the deeds of the Lord. God always acts in accordance with his justice, which is part of his nature.

This is celebrated in numerous psalms such as Psalm 71 which pleads, *"Rescue me and deliver me in your righteousness"* (tsadaq – justice) . . . *"My mouth will tell of your righteousness (tsadaq – justice), of your salvation all day long, though I know not its measure. I will come and proclaim your mighty acts, O Sovereign Lord; I will proclaim your righteousness (tsadaq – justice), yours alone"* (verses 15 and 16).

God's Acts Show His Justice

In order to understand God's justice, we need to study the history of Israel which shows the way he dealt with the nation with whom he formed a covenant relationship. The covenant played a central part in that history. When the people of Israel kept the terms of the covenant, they enjoyed peace and prosperity, in marked contrast to when they broke the terms of the covenant and disaster came upon them. In the times when Israel was in a right relationship with God they were able to sing of his goodness and faithfulness which we see in many of the Psalms, such as:

"Great is the Lord and most worthy of praise; his greatness no one can fathom . . . I will meditate on your wonderful works. They will tell of the power of your awesome works, and I will proclaim your great deeds. They will celebrate your abundant goodness and joyfully sing of your righteousness (tsadaq – justice)" (Ps 145:3-7).

There were other times when things were not going well but God's justice is seen in his acts of saving the oppressed. *"He will judge the world in righteousness; he will govern the peoples with justice. The Lord is a refuge for the oppressed, a stronghold in times of trouble. Those who know your name will trust you, for you, Lord, have never forsaken those who seek you"* (Ps 9:8-10). God's supreme act of saving the oppressed is to be seen in the way he delivered the Hebrew slaves from Egypt.

In our Western understanding we think of justice as giving everyone exactly what they deserve – 'distributive justice'. But such a concept is quite foreign to Hebraic teaching. God's justice often defies human logic, and this is celebrated in Psalm 103:

"The Lord works righteousness and justice for all the oppressed. He made known his ways to Moses, his deeds to the people of Israel . . . He does not treat us as our sins deserve or repay us according to our iniquities. For as high as the heavens are above the earth, so great is his love for those who fear him" (Ps 103:6-11).

This statement is of supreme importance in understanding the justice of God. The teaching of the prophets is fully in line with this, as Isaiah emphasised:

"As the heavens are higher than the earth, so are my ways higher than your ways and my thoughts than your thoughts . . . So is my word that goes out from my mouth: it will not return to me empty, but will accomplish what I desire and achieve the purpose for which I sent it" (Is 55:9-11).

Hebraic Understanding of Justice

The Hebrew word *tsadaq* is usually translated as either 'justice' or 'righteousness'. Righteousness is the word favoured in many English translations, especially in the New Testament. The Authorised Version of the New Testament does not contain the word justice; yet in recent years there has been a distinct movement among theologians to emphasise the Hebraic roots of the New Testament. This is giving increasing recognition to the value of translating Paul's use of *dikaiosunē* in Romans, as 'justice' rather than 'righteousness' – in fact it gives a whole new understanding to his teaching – as for example, the context demands in Romans 6:13. What does Paul mean by "instruments of righteousness"? As a Hebrew Rabbi Paul would have been thinking in terms of using our lives to create right relationships with others and being in a right relationship with God which would demand translating this as "instruments of *justice*".

It is worth reading through Romans and substituting the word 'justice' for 'righteousness'. This takes away the concept of *morality* associated with righteousness in Western culture, and allows the Hebraic interpretation of Paul's thoughts to be revealed, for example, in Romans 3:20 where Paul says, *"Therefore no one will be declared righteous in his sight by observing the law"*. Paul certainly is not referring to morality. He is speaking about being in a *right relationship* with God, which is the concept he would have been taught when he learnt the *Torah* from Rabbi Gamaliel.

In the Old Testament, *tsadaq* – 'justice', and *mishpat* – 'judgment' are almost invariably related to relationships. They refer to the relationship between God and human beings; but they also refer to relationships *between* human beings. Thus, the just man or woman is the person who is in a right relationship with God and with their neighbours. This involves both vertical and horizontal relationships. When these are right, the relationship can be said to be 'just'. A good example is in Proverbs 16:11, *"Honest scales and balances are from the Lord"*. Here *mishpat* is used to describe the weights on a scale being in perfect harmony. They are described as "honest scales" because they are 'just' and 'right' before the Lord.

Similarly, *tsadaq* is used in Deuteronomy 32:4 to describe both the actions and the nature of God: *"He is the Rock, his works are perfect, and all his ways are just. A faithful God who does no wrong, upright and just is he."* And in Psalm 89:14 it is said, *"Righteousness and justice are the foundation of your throne."*

Justice in the New Testament

When we turn to the New Testament, we have only one word, *dikaios* meaning 'just' and 'upright'; as in Matthew 1:19 where it is said that Joseph, Mary's husband was a 'just' or 'upright' man. This is unfortunately translated in most English Bibles as *"a righteous man"* which implies that he was morally a good man and this sets the precedent for the use of *dikaios* throughout the New Testament.

In a wider meaning of justice, the same concept can be applied to the right ordering of things in the world; so that there is a right ordering in the cosmos, or in all created things. In the Bible this concept is applied to such things as weights and measures. The just man will be using weights that are true and trustworthy: hence the injunction, *"Do not use dishonest standards when measuring length, weight or quantity. Use honest scales and honest weights, an honest epher and an honest hin. I am the Lord your God, who brought you out of Egypt"* (Lev 19:35-36).

Amos charged the merchants in the market with *"cheating with dishonest scales"* (Am 7:5). Such actions were not simply dishonest, they were unjust; and injustice destroyed community relationships. The prophets all railed against injustice. It was one of the six sins of Jerusalem featured in Jeremiah's famous temple sermon (Jer 7). Amos said that the religious feasts and festivals of Israel were unacceptable to God. He said, *"Away with the noise of your songs! I will not listen to the music of your harps. But let justice roll on like a river, righteousness like a never-failing stream!"* (Am 5:23-24).

Western Justice and Roman Law

Western concepts of justice have come, not from Hebraic teaching but from Roman law. In Roman law, justice is rooted in punishing offenders strictly in accordance with the offence. It would seem fundamentally unjust in Roman law to deal with an offender in any other way, although under certain circumstances the exercise of mercy could be considered. But to say to a persistent offender that his offences have been totally erased would be unthinkable. Yet this is in fact what is said in the prophets. *"Though your sins are like scarlet they shall be as white as snow"* (Is 1:18) and Isaiah himself was given the personal assurance *"Your guilt is taken away and your sin atoned for"* (Is 6:7).

Similarly, in Paul's teaching in 1 Corinthians 13:5 he makes the statement, *"Love keeps no record of wrongs"*. When God forgives, he forgives completely and wipes the record clean. He does not leave it on the back burner in order to raise the issue again at some later date, as we so often do in our human relationships.

God's Covenant Promise

It is even more remarkable that in Hebraic thinking such an action of forgiveness is seen as God exercising justice! This is because justice is part of God's nature and he must be true to himself. This is clearly stated in 2 Timothy 2:13, *"If we are faithless, he will remain faithful, for he cannot disown himself"*. God is always faithful to his covenant promises. His covenant promises are not bilateral as in an agreement between two parties. The covenant God makes is one that he decrees with his chosen people to whom he promises to watch over for their good in order to fulfil his purposes through them.

Therefore, when God exercises lovingkindness and forgiveness to a rebellious people, he is actually being true to himself, in fulfilling his covenant promises, regardless of the cost to himself. When Jeremiah received the revelation of God's intention to make a new covenant *"with the house of Israel"* God reaffirmed his covenant promise, *"I will be their God and they will be my people"*. He also made a solemn promise, *"Only if the heavens above can be measured and the foundations of the earth below be searched out, will I reject all the descendants of Israel, because of all they have done, declares the Lord"* (Jer 31:37). God's covenant promise is unconditional. It is irrespective of the faithfulness or unfaithfulness of his people. God has to be true to himself, and in Hebraic terms this is God's justice: being just to himself: being in a right relationship with himself: maintaining harmony within his nature.

Justice and Mercy in fulfilling God's Covenant Promises

There were many times in the history of Israel when God exercised mercy that was entirely unmerited, but in so doing he was being true to himself: he was exercising his own kind of justice. It is this concept of justice that runs right through the promises in Isaiah 61, a passage of Scripture that Jesus read and developed in the synagogue at Nazareth (Luke 4:16). These promises are based upon the statement, *"For I, the Lord, love justice, I hate robbery and iniquity. In my faithfulness I will reward them and make an everlasting covenant with them. Their descendants will be known among the nations and their offspring among the peoples. All who see them will acknowledge that they are the people the Lord has blessed"* (Is 61:8-9). In fulfilling his covenant promises God's nature would be revealed to the world.

God's justice can be seen to be tender towards the poor and distressed. It was for this reason that he listened to the cries of his people in slavery in Egypt. With no consideration of their moral or spiritual credit, God reached out his hand and saved his people from oppression. Time after time the saving act in the history of Israel is remembered by the prophets, psalmists and historians, and it is celebrated as an act of God's justice. Psalm 78 records some of the history of Israel and notes the times when the people rebelled against God, but still he was faithful to his covenant promises.

This is recorded in Psalm 105:8, *"He remembers his covenant for ever, the word he commanded, for a thousand generations, the covenant he made with Abraham, the oath he swore to Isaac."* In Psalm 106, after it is recorded that God saved them from their enemies (verses 8-13) we have in verses 13-14: *"But they soon forgot what he had done and did not wait for his counsel. In the desert they gave into their craving; in the wasteland they put God to the test."* However, in verse 44 the Psalmist states, *"But he took note of their distress when he heard their cries; for their sake he remembered his covenant and out of his great love he relented."* This is God's justice. It is God being true to himself.

Justice in the Teaching of Jesus

The teaching of Jesus on justice is fully in line with the use of the word in the Old Testament. The Beatitudes turn upside down logical concepts of justice. It is the poor in spirit who inherit the kingdom; and the meek, not the powerful, who inherit the earth. The values of the kingdom turn the values of the world upside down. The kind of justice that Jesus teaches surprises everyone; just as God's justice does in the teaching of the prophets, like fulfilling his covenant promises to care for his people, despite all the wicked things they do.

In his parables, Jesus teaches justice that is outside the law such as the employer who pays a latecomer a full day's wages, which outraged the legalists in the crowd. Most shocking of all, he described the father whose wastrel son had squandered his inheritance and yet was received back by the father and treated as a hero! Jesus was emphasising that God does not treat us as we deserve, and in all his teaching he opposes the 'eye for an eye' concept of justice. His followers were not to repay persecution and hatred with violence, but with loving forbearance, turning the other cheek to aggressors.

Justice in the teaching of Jesus was not in the language of the legal transaction, but in the language of love. It was good news for the poor, the oppressed, the blind and the prisoner. The kind of justice Jesus taught does not retaliate when struck, but returns love for hatred and good for evil. This is the essence of the Hebraic understanding of God's justice, revealed by the prophets of Israel from the 8th to the 6th century BC but it was this teaching that was lost in the westernisation of the Bible. The Western theologians who followed in the steps of Luther, who was steeped in anti-Semitism, turned a blind eye to the Hebraic roots of the faith and in so doing they lost the gospel of Jesus and they twisted the teaching of Paul, the master Hebraic theologian, making his teaching conform to Roman law.

The Western Church

In the Western church today the Hebraic roots of the Christian faith are often not recognised, due to the neglect of the Old Testament. This is especially true of the newer denominations where there is no observation of a liturgy that requires systematic reading of the whole Bible.

The Western church today is largely a reflection of Western civilisation and culture but what is often not recognised is the degree to which the church has been responsible for influencing the development of that very civilisation and culture by which it is now enslaved. The social process of secularisation that has produced the present situation was largely set in train by sterile biblical enquiry.

Scholarship without faith does not get into the mind of God: it falls at the first hurdle – *"as the heavens are higher than the earth, so are my ways higher than your ways and my thoughts than your thoughts"* (Is 55:9). Without the Hebraic key to unlock the treasures of the Hebrew Scriptures, we can never discover the truth or enter into what Jeremiah describes as *"The council of the Lord"* (Jer 23:18).

At root, anti-Semitism, which has been embraced by most branches of the Western church, has been hugely influential in the development of the culture of Western nations. The church in the West has a long history of persecuting Jews that goes right back to the time when the Emperor Constantine banned Jewish believers from attending the Council of Nicaea in 325 AD. This meant that there were no Hebrew speakers at the influential church council who could have brought an Hebraic concept to the dispute between Arius and Athanasius.

Since that day, the church in the West has moved steadily away from its biblical roots, resulting in a loss of a Hebraic understanding of justice, which is central to the nature of God. Constantine was strongly anti-Jewish and he deliberately moved the church away from celebrating Hebrew festivals including moving Easter away from Passover and changing the 'sabbath' from Saturday to Sunday, which was his holy day, as he was a sun worshipper before embracing Christianity.

The concept that the Christian church has replaced Israel in the purposes of God, or 'Replacement Theology', could only arise among theologians who fail to understand the nature of God and his commitment to keeping his covenant promises. Hostile attitudes towards Jews in the Western nations were responsible for numerous massacres such as that in the city of York in 1190 AD and for the expulsion of Jews from Spain in 1492 AD. But it was Luther who indelibly planted anti-Semitism at the heart of the Protestant Reformation. Although he was initially friendly towards the Jews, when he was hoping that they would embrace Protestant Christianity, he later changed his attitude.

Luther

In his book *Concerning the Jews and their Lies* Luther advised his followers to eradicate Jewish homes and synagogues by burning them to the ground and covering the site with dirt. Prayer books and Talmuds were to be destroyed, rabbis silenced on pain of death, travel forbidden, wealth seized and usually impounded; young Jews were to be enslaved at harsh tasks. As a final step, Luther advocated the expulsion; "Let us drive them out of the country for all time" he concluded, "To sum up, dear princes and nobles who have Jews in your domains, if this advice of mine does not suit you, then find a better one so that you and we may all be free of this insufferable devilish burden – the Jews."[4]

It is well-known that Adolf Hitler based a lot of his thinking upon Luther's teaching. This led to the unspeakable atrocities of the central European Holocaust and the murder of 6 million Jews in Nazi concentration camps. The Western Protestant churches have never acknowledged the extent of their responsibility for the Holocaust, and Replacement Theology is still rife in Western churches.

---

4   Martin Luther, quoted in Richard E Grade, *A Historical Survey of Anti-Semitism*, Baker Book House, Grand Rapids, 1981, page 51.

Distributive Justice

The false theology at the heart of Replacement Theology is rooted in disputes which go right back to the Early Church and the struggle for power between East and West in which the influence of Hebrew Christianity became lost. The Roman church triumphed in the West which resulted in the adoption of the Latin definition of law as 'distributive justice'.

This became the basic understanding of justice for interpreting references throughout the Bible. The 18th century publication of Cruden's Concordance, first published in London 1737, gives a definition of 'justice' as *"that political virtue that renders to every man his due and is distributive justice."* This shows the extent to which the Roman concept of justice had been accepted throughout the Western churches and had become embedded in the culture.

CHAPTER 4

THE DEEDS OF THE LORD

A God of Action

An outstanding characteristic of the Bible, from Genesis to Revelation, is that it is a record of the 'deeds of the Lord'. It presents a God of *action* – from the act of creation of the universe through to the revelation of the last days – God is active! He is active throughout history, both in the natural creation and in the affairs of humanity. He did not create the universe and retire into obscure inactivity; he continues to be active in his creation from generation to generation.

The Bible also provides a record of the progressive revelation of God – from Adam to Jesus, in each generation God adds to our knowledge of him. This self-revelation climaxes in the advent of Messiah Jesus and concludes with the promise of his return. In this chapter we explore the writings of the prophets of Israel that reveal the nature and purposes of God.

Faith and Trust

In Deuteronomy 3 there is an account of a conversation between God and Moses that shows the intimacy of their relationship. It is especially revealing in showing the level of trust that Moses had acquired from the time he left Egypt to the day he stood on the top of Mount Nebo and looked across the Jordan to the land of Canaan.

Moses had longed to enter the land promised to his ancestor Abraham more than four centuries earlier and he had endured untold sufferings, tests, and setbacks in leading the people of Israel for 40 years through the desert. But God did not allow him to cross the Jordan. That task was given to Joshua. Moses had accomplished all that God had required of him. A new man was now needed for the new phase in God's dealings with his people.

Joshua was a man of immense courage and through his close relationship with Moses and the experience of seeing the amazing things that God did during those 40 years in the wilderness, Joshua was able to trust God in an extraordinary way – even when God told him to do things that defy human logic, such as walking round the walls of Jericho for seven days. Joshua had learned that God could be completely trusted to carry out what he said he would do.

It was this trust in God which generated the faith commended in Hebrews 11, noting the men and women in the history of Israel who achieved great things by their faith. That faith in the God of their fathers, Abraham, Isaac and Jacob, came from a knowledge of the constancy and trustworthiness of God – that his nature was unchanging and totally reliable. He was not a capricious god like the gods of the pagan religions worshipped by other people groups. If God gave a promise it would be fulfilled.

The One and Only God

When God declared he would do something, he had the power to accomplish it. This was the message given to Isaiah:

"I have revealed and saved and proclaimed – I, and not some foreign god among you. You are my witnesses, declares the Lord, that I am God. Yes, and from ancient days I am he. No one can deliver out of my hand. When I act, who can reverse it?" (Is 43:12-13).

It was this message that came as a fresh revelation to the people who were enslaved in Babylon. They had to be convinced that the God of their fathers was the one and only God. There was no other. He was the God of Creation who was enthroned above the circle of the earth, who stretched out the heavens like a canopy, and held the nations in his hands like a drop in the bucket (Is 40:15). Isaiah had to convince the people that the God of Israel was not only the Creator of the Universe, but that he was the one and only God.

"To whom will you compare me? Or who is my equal? Says the Holy One. Lift up your eyes and look to the heavens; who created all these? He who brings out the starry host one by one, and calls them each by name" (Is 40:25-26).

Isaiah went on to say that God was not only the One who created the universe but that he was also the **Sustainer** of Creation. He was the one who had flung the stars into orbit, but he was still active in his creation. *"Because of his great power and mighty strength, not one of them is missing"*. He continued, *"The Lord is the everlasting God, the Creator of the ends of the earth. He will not grow tired or weary, and his understanding no one can fathom. He gives strength to the weary and increases the power of the weak"* (Is 40:26-29).

The Holiness of God

All these statements were preparing the ground for the declaration that God was about to break the power of the Babylonian Empire and release his people from slavery, to return to the promised land and rebuild the shattered city of Jerusalem. This was a momentous message coming to a people who were now in the third generation of their exile in Babylon. By this time few of them spoke Hebrew and most of them had adjusted in their daily lives to living in Babylon. Some of them had even abandoned the faith of their forefathers and fallen into doing the same idolatrous practices as their Babylonian neighbours, even sacrificing their babies.

God had raised up the young Ezekiel to be the anointed teacher of the first exiles in Babylon. Ezekiel had been taken from Jerusalem where he had been born into one of the aristocratic priestly families, although as he was under 30 years of age he probably had not begun to minister in the temple. But he would have had an education as a priest, so he would have been familiar with the history of the nation and the teaching of Moses. He was in one of the first waves of exiles in 596 BC, but it was five years later that he had an experience of the living God that changed his life and God commissioned him as a prophet to the exiles.

The elders from the village settlements scattered around Babylonia used to come regularly to sit at the feet of Ezekiel, to listen to his teaching and to ask if there was any word from the Lord. On one occasion Ezekiel berated them:

"This is what the Sovereign Lord says: 'Will you defile yourselves the way your fathers did and lust after their vile images? When you offer your gifts – the sacrifice of your sons in the fire – you continue to defile yourselves with all the idols to this day. Am I to let you enquire with me, O house of Israel? As surely as I live, declares the Sovereign Lord, I will not let you enquire of me" (Ezek 20:30-31).

The pressures to conform to the social standards of the people of Babylon must have been immense upon the people of Judah. For the first 10 years of the exile they would have been relying upon the daily prayers being said in the temple in Jerusalem on their behalf and they also had plenty of false prophets among them who were telling them that any day God was going to do something miraculous and overthrow Babylon and allow the people to go back home. Jeremiah had to counter these lies and say that the prophets among them had not been sent by God. *"For they have not listened to my words, declares the Lord, words that I sent to them again and again by my servants the prophets. And you exiles have not listened either, declares the Lord"* (Jer 29:19).

The God of Truth

The social pressures upon the exiles increased enormously after 586 AD when Jerusalem was destroyed by the Babylonians and a further wave of exiles from Judah were brought to Babylon with their tales of horror and all that they had seen. They may even have brought with them copies of the words of Jeremiah and maybe even a scroll of Lamentations. The news of Jerusalem's fall was a bitter blow to the exiles as recorded in Ezekiel 24:

"Say to the house of Israel, this is what the Sovereign Lord says: I am about to desecrate my sanctuary – the stronghold in which you take pride, the delight of your eyes, the object of your affection. The sons and daughters you left behind will fall by the sword" (Ezek 24:21).

It was essential for God to allow Jerusalem to be destroyed and then also the temple. This took away all the human institutions in which the people put their trust. It was the institutional religion at the temple that had become a vessel of deception, based upon the false beliefs and prophecies given to the people by the priests and prophets in Jerusalem. Jeremiah spent a lifetime countering these false beliefs and declaring that these men had not been sent by God and were deceiving the people.

"From the least to the greatest all are greedy for gain; prophets and priests alike all practice deceit. They dress the wound of my people as though it were not serious. Peace, peace they say when there is no peace" (Jer 6:13).

False Prophecies and Deception

Jeremiah pleaded with the people not to listen to their religious leaders: *"Do not listen to what the prophets are prophesying to you; they fill you with false hopes. They speak visions from their own minds, and not from the mouth of the Lord"* (Jer 23:16). The devastating effect of these false religious beliefs was that the people were all convinced that no enemy would be allowed to enter the city of Jerusalem and no foreigner would be able to enter the temple because God would strike them down.

The great problem that Jeremiah faced was that the people all knew from the history of Israel, the great things that God had done in the past. Not only had he performed miracles in the time of Moses and forced the Egyptians to release the people of Israel from slavery in Egypt, but in more recent years God had actually performed miracles to save Jerusalem in the time of King Jehoshaphat, and even more recently in the time of King Hezekiah, when the mighty Assyrian army had been routed by plague outside the walls of Jerusalem.

The people knew the power of God, so it was easy to spread deception and false teaching among them. The myth of the inviolability of the temple in Jerusalem became a central tenet in the religion of the people, reinforced by the preaching and teaching of the priests and prophets. They taught that the temple was the dwelling of God, so he would always protect it against foreign invasion. This dangerous teaching ignored the irrevocable conditions in the covenant relationship between God and Israel that required them to worship no other God. It also ignored the revelation of the justice of God that had been given through earlier prophets such as Amos who had declared:

"I hate, I despise your religious feasts; I cannot stand your assemblies. Even though you bring me burnt offerings and grain offerings, I will not accept them. Though you bring choice fellowship offerings, I will have no regard for them. Away with the noise of your songs! I will not listen to the music of your harps. But let justice roll on like a river, righteousness like a never-failing stream!" (Am 5:22- 24).

The Justice of God

What the people of Judah did not understand was the nature of God and the terms of the covenant that had been established with Moses. They did not understand that God's promises were conditional upon the obedience of the people and their total trust in him, demonstrated by their abhorrence of idols and their freedom from all idolatrous practices. This was declared by Jeremiah in the temple and outside the temple and everywhere else in the streets of the city to whoever would listen to him. His famous Temple Sermon recorded in Jeremiah 7 concluded with the words:

"When I brought your forefathers out of Egypt and spoke to them, I did not just give them commands about burnt offerings and sacrifices, but I gave them this command: obey me, and I will be your God and you will be my people. Walk in all the ways I command you, that it may go well with you. But they did not listen or pay attention; instead, they followed the stubborn inclinations of their evil hearts. They went backward and not forward. From the time your forefathers left Egypt until now, day after day, again and again I sent you my servants the prophets. But they did not listen to me or pay attention. They were stiff-necked and did more evil than their forefathers" (Jer 7:22-26).

There was really no excuse for the false teachings of the priests and prophets in Jerusalem because Moses himself had stressed the need for obedience. Time after time he warned the people that if they got into idolatry, disobeying the first commandment that they should have no other God than Yahweh, the promises of protection that God made in his covenant would become null and void. Deuteronomy 28 spelt out, not only the blessings for obedience, but also the curses for disobedience.

"If you do not obey the Lord your God and you do not carefully follow all his commands and decrees I am giving you today, all these curses will come upon you and overtake you" (Deut 28:15).

Warnings

The rest of Deuteronomy 28 sets out in detail the curses that would come upon the nation as a result of disobedience. Moses said:

"If you do not carefully follow all the words of this law, which are written in this book, and do not revere this glorious and awesome name – the Lord your God – the Lord will send fearful plagues on you and

your descendants, harsh and prolonged disasters . . . Just as it pleased the Lord to make you prosper and increase in number, so it will please him to ruin and destroy you. You will be uprooted from the land you are entering to possess" (Deut 28:58-63).

That final word saying that it would *"please God"* to ruin and destroy the people of Israel, his covenant people, is surely a poor translation. The true meaning is that God would not hesitate to carry out his word even though he knew that it would bring terrible suffering to the people whom he loved. The justice in the nature of God demanded that he should be true to himself. But God's justice always has to be seen alongside his love. This was the dilemma that God faced throughout the history of his dealings with Israel. It is beautifully described by the Prophet Hosea:

How can I give you up, Ephraim? How can I hand you over, Israel? . . . My heart is changed within me; all my compassion is aroused. I will not carry out my fierce anger, nor will I turn and devastate Ephraim. For I am God and not man – the Holy One among you. I will not come in wrath" (Hos 11:1-9).

The Love of God

It is almost certain that Jeremiah was familiar with the scroll of Hosea who preceded him, ministering as a prophet in Jerusalem during the reign of Hezekiah. Scrolls of his writings would have been kept in the temple and it may be that Jeremiah was remembering the passage quoted above when he said: *"The Lord appeared to us in the past, saying: I have loved you with an everlasting love; I have drawn you with loving kindness. I will build you up again and you will be rebuilt, O Virgin Israel. Again, you will take up your tambourines and go out to dance with the joyful"* (Jer 31:3-4).

It is quite wrong to think of Jeremiah as a miserable man always proclaiming doom and gloom. He was a realist: and he had a revelation of the nature and purposes of God that was quite outstanding – it is a revelation that is as greatly needed today as it was in the time of Jeremiah when there was not only widespread idolatry but also adultery, family breakdown, many different forms of immorality such as bribery and corruption plus injustice and oppression, with violence and murder on the streets of Jerusalem. All these things are referred to in Jeremiah's famous 'Temple Sermon' in chapter 7 where, in a brilliant piece of oratory from the steps outside the temple he said:

"Will you steal and murder, commit adultery and perjury, burn incense to Baal and follow other gods you have not known, and then come and stand before me in this house, which bears my name, and say, 'We are safe' – safe to do all these detestable things? Has this house, which bears my Name, become a den of robbers to you? But I have been watching! declares the Lord" (Jer 7:9-11).

Love and Justice

The characteristics of the nature of God, that were revealed to Jeremiah early in his ministry, showed the mixture of love and justice in the character of God. This is what Hosea had perceived:

"When Israel was a child, I loved him, and out of Israel I called my son. But the more I called Israel, the further he went from me… It was I who taught Ephraim to walk, taking them by the arms; but they did not realise it was I who healed them. I led them with chords of human kindness and ties of love" (Hos 11:1-4).

Hosea perceived the distress in the heart of God that the people did not realise all the wonderful things that God had done for them. He had not only led them through the wilderness and into the promised land, but he had protected them and had healed their diseases. He had prospered them and provided them with food, but they went to the high places and thanked Baal whom the Canaanites said was the owner of the land. They did not realise that the God of Israel, the Creator of the Universe, was the owner of the land and provided them with food. He led them with *"chords of human kindness and with ties of love"*, but they turned their backs and spurned his love.

A Covenant Keeping God

Jeremiah faced the widespread idolatry that had been introduced by Manasseh and his son Amon. It had spread among the people and led to all kinds of immoral and licentious behaviour that was deeply grieving to God. What he also perceived was that God is a covenant-keeping God, but in order for God to keep his covenant promises to protect his people, they had to be faithful in having no other God and putting their trust solely in the God of their fathers.

From the day of his call to ministry Jeremiah was aware of danger on the international horizon. He had seen a boiling pot, tilting away from the North, and God had said that he was rightly discerning the danger, *"From the North disaster will be poured out on all who live in the land"* (Jer 1:14).

God went farther than simply confirming that Jeremiah was right in recognising the danger from Babylon, which was a greater threat than Assyria whose empire was on the wane. But God said something far more significant and threatening than the spectre of two rival empires seeking to dominate the region. **The danger was from God himself losing patience with his covenant people who were worshipping other gods, and were actually breaking the terms of that covenant themselves.** This was the fear that gripped Jeremiah's heart, because he knew that the God of Israel was a covenant keeping God.

What God actually said was: *"I am about to summon all the peoples of the northern kingdoms."* He said they would come and lay siege to the city of Jerusalem. But instead of promising that he would protect the city, God said **"I will pronounce judgments on my people because of their wickedness in forsaking me,** *in burning incense to other gods and in worshipping what their hands have made"* (Jer 1:15-16).

So, from the beginning of his ministry Jeremiah knew that unless there was repentance in the nation and turning away from idolatry, God would not defend Jerusalem against invasion. He was so sure he had rightly heard God speaking to him, that it fixed the pattern of his ministry for the rest of his life. For Jeremiah, conveying the danger to the leaders of the nation and the people of Jerusalem became a passion. He wrote:

"Oh, my anguish, my anguish! I writhed in pain. Oh, the agony of my heart! My heart pounds within me, I cannot keep silent. For I have heard the sound of the trumpet; I have heard the battle cry" (Jer 4:19).

Jeremiah saw, in a vision, the whole land devastated, with the fruitful land a desert and the towns in ruins. It was the certainty of this tragedy becoming a reality, unless there was repentance and turning, that drove him for the rest of his ministry in Jerusalem.

Loyalty and Trust

The outstanding truth that was revealed to Jeremiah at the beginning of his ministry was that God was not only a covenant-keeping God who longed to bless his people with peace and prosperity, but that he was also a God who demanded loyalty and who expected his people to trust him completely. Although this was not a new revelation, because it had been there from the time the covenant was sealed with the 'Great Assembly' (Ex 19:17) at the foot of Mount Sinai when the law was given to Moses, it had never really been fully embraced by the people of Israel and Judah.

In Jeremiah's day the religious life of the nation was in a terrible mess with the people fraternising with the Canaanites and worshipping their gods at the high places across the land of Judah. There were totem poles and other symbols of their Baal worship that were detestable to the God of Israel, and there were even shrines to other gods in the streets of Jerusalem.

When King Josiah carried out a programme of repairs in the temple that led to the discovery of a scroll containing the Ten Commandments, it led the king to carry out a programme of reform. The scroll contained much of the teaching given by God through Moses, which led Josiah to call the whole nation to repentance and to reaffirm the covenant with God. Jeremiah warmly applauded the reforms carried out by the King. In fact, he went farther saying: *"Cursed is the man who does not obey the terms of this covenant – the terms I commanded your forefathers when I brought them out of Egypt"* (Jer 11:3).

It was not that Jeremiah revelled in destruction, quite the reverse, he recoiled at what he knew was coming upon the people. *"Oh, that my head were a spring of water and my eyes a fountain of tears! I would weep day and night for the slain of my people"* (Jer 9.1).

The whole Book of Lamentations with its descriptions of the horror left behind by the cruelty of the Babylonian warriors either comes directly from Jeremiah or from his disciples. It attempts to express the inexpressible suffering that God had allowed to happen: *"Without pity the Lord has swallowed up all the dwellings of Jacob; in his wrath he has torn down the strongholds of the daughter of Judah. He has brought her kingdom and its princes down to the ground in dishonour."* Of course, Jeremiah suffered. *"My eyes fail with weeping I am in torment within, my heart is poured out to the ground because my people are destroyed"* (Lam 2:2 and 11).

The whole of Jeremiah's ministry was devoted to attempting to prevent the catastrophe that happened in 586 BC. He knew that it would not happen if there were repentance and turning in the nation. He was still calling for repentance when the Babylonians were outside the city because he knew what had happened in the time of the righteous King Hezekiah when he and the Prophet Isaiah had gone into the temple and spread before the Lord the threatening letter from the Assyrian commander and God had responded to their request sending a plague overnight sweeping through the besieging army that killed 185,000 men.

A God of Purpose

Of course, Jeremiah knew that God would respond immediately to a repentant nation. But he also knew that it was God's intention to use the men and women who had been sent to Babylon for a special purpose. They were to be transformed into a company of redeemed believers who would return to Jerusalem and prepare the way for the coming of Messiah. This was revealed to Jeremiah, as often happened, through an everyday event which God used to speak to him.

When Jerusalem surrendered in 597 BC, the Babylonians rounded up a huge band of captives, including the king and his family, and the whole army of Judah to take to Babylon. Soon after they left, Jeremiah was walking past the temple in what was now the sparsely occupied streets of the city. There on the steps in front of the temple were two baskets of figs. One basket had very good figs that looked mouth-wateringly ripe, while the other basket had figs that were so bad they could not be eaten. The Lord spoke to Jeremiah, what do you see? *"Figs,"* he said. And then the Lord revealed his reason for allowing the Babylonians to conquer Jerusalem and take so many of its leading citizens and others from the surrounding villages.

God said: *"Like these good figs, I regard as good all the exiles from Judah, whom I sent away from this place to the land of the Babylonians. My eyes will watch over them for their good, and I will bring them back to this land. I will build them up and not tear them down; I will plant them and not uproot them. I will give them a heart to know me, that I am the Lord. They will be my people and I will be their God, for they will return to me with all their heart"* (Jer 24:5-7).

This revelation was no doubt a tremendous comfort to Jeremiah who had spent many years calling for repentance in the nation, pleading with the King and his political advisers as well as with the priests and other leaders in the nation. He knew that God would not defend an unrighteous people who had no trust in him.

Jeremiah's Scroll

In 604 BC, some eight years before the Babylonian invasion, Jeremiah had ordered Baruch his amanuensis to take a new scroll and write on it all the words that God had spoken to him since the reign of Josiah warning of disaster, and sent them to Jehoiakim following his father's untimely death some four years earlier. But King Jehoiakim had no fear of the Lord. As each section of the scroll was read to him, the King took his knife and cut it from the scroll, throwing it into the brazier until the entire scroll was burned in the fire. This was despite many protests from his courtiers.

Jeremiah was then told to take another scroll and to write on it all the words that were on the original scroll and to add many more. It was probably soon after that, that Jeremiah received the revelation recorded in chapter 31, that the day would come when God would make a 'new covenant' with the house of Israel and with the house of Judah which would not be like the original covenant made in the time of Moses, which the people were despising. God was looking forward to the time when he could make a new covenant that would be on an entirely different basis. He said:

"I will put my law in their minds and write it on their hearts. I will be their God and they will be my people. No longer will a man teach his neighbour, or a man his brother, saying know the Lord, because they will all know me from the least of them to the greatest declares the Lord" (Jer 31:33-34).

The Message of the Figs

God had also used the two baskets of figs to speak to Jeremiah about the people remaining in Jerusalem, likening them to the poor-quality figs in saying that they would be subject to the sword, famine and plague. But this did not stop Jeremiah from calling for repentance and change: it simply sharpened his message of warnings to the people. Jeremiah was horrified when he discovered that King

Zedekiah was plotting with neighbouring countries to revolt against Babylon despite the fact that he had sworn an oath of loyalty in the name of Yahweh the God of Israel.

Jeremiah even made a public demonstration of his message by having a yoke of crossbars and straps on his shoulders, walking around the streets of Jerusalem and saying that this is what was going to happen to all the people: they will be taken into servitude if Zedekiah went ahead with his planned revolt. He took the opportunity of denouncing the religious leaders in Jerusalem who were still declaring that they would never come under the yoke of the king of Babylon. He sent the same message of warning to the king, saying *"Do not listen to the words of the prophets who say to you, you will not serve the king of Babylon, for they are prophesying lies to you. 'I have not sent them', declares the Lord"* (Jer 27:14).

Those two baskets of figs were a turning point in Jeremiah's ministry enabling him to perceive the purposes of God in allowing the Babylonians to prevail over Judah and to take so many people into exile in Babylon. Once he understood the purpose of God, his objective was to save those remaining in Jerusalem from the disaster he knew would befall them if they did not put their trust in the Lord. Once Zedekiah put into practice his threatened revolt, Jeremiah realised that the fate of the city was sealed.

News that the Babylonian army was advancing towards Jerusalem caused the Egyptians to mobilise their army and begin to come to the aid of Judah in accordance with an earlier agreement. The Babylonian army then withdrew from Jerusalem and began marching south to meet the Egyptians who then turned and ran for home. Jeremiah had already perceived that this withdrawal was only a temporary lull. The message he sent to the king was:

"This is what the Lord says: do not deceive yourselves, thinking, the Babylonians will surely leave us. They will not! Even if you were to defeat the entire Babylonian army that is attacking you and only wounded men were left in their tents, they would come and burn the city down" (Jer 37:10).

This statement illustrates the degree of certainty that Jeremiah had that it was God's purpose to nurture and redeem the exiles in Babylon and that they would be the ones who God would use to work out his purposes for the future of the nation and the preservation of the faith of the people of Israel.

A God of Forgiveness

Until the time of Zedekiah's foolish revolt against Babylon, Jeremiah was still calling for repentance. Once news reached Jerusalem that the Babylonian army was on the march, Jeremiah knew that the fate of Jerusalem was sealed. There was no further point in calling for repentance and turning. Of course, he knew that God is a God of forgiveness and that many times he had relented of bringing judgment upon the people of Israel for their sins. He undoubtedly would have known about the times Moses had stood in the presence of the Lord pleading on behalf of the people. It was one of the well-known stories in the history of Israel of how the people had made a golden calf when Moses was up the mountain receiving the Ten Commandments.

Jeremiah's boyhood education in the family of a priest at Anathoth would have included a graphic account of this incident when it was reported that Aaron had let the people get out of control so that they had become a laughing stock to their enemies. But Moses laid his own eternal salvation on the line pleading with God for the forgiveness of the people. He said *"Oh, what a great sin these people have committed! They have made themselves gods of gold. But now, please forgive their sin – but if not, then blot me out of the book you have written"* (Ex 32:31-32).

It was no doubt the fact that God did forgive the people, not only on this single occasion but on many more that Moses perceived that forgiveness was part of the very nature of God. He said, **"The Lord is slow to anger, abounding in love and forgiving sin and rebellion"** (Num 14:18a). This became part of the spiritual tradition of the people of Israel, passed on from generation to generation. It is quoted by Daniel in his famous prayer. *"The Lord our God is merciful and forgiving, even though we have rebelled against him"* (Dan 9:9).

It was no doubt Jeremiah's confidence in forgiveness being part of the nature of God that accounted for the confidence with which he spoke of the restoration of the exiles in Babylon and the rebuilding of the city of Jerusalem at the end of the exile.

During the two-year siege of Jerusalem by the Babylonian army which created a situation of unbearable suffering among the people inside the city, Jeremiah, who had been caught trying to leave the city before the siege, was imprisoned in the guardhouse. It was during this time that he was told by the Lord to purchase a field in his home territory of Anathoth which was no doubt already in enemy occupied territory. He did this, making a public show of his signing the deed of purchase and sealing it in a jar where it could be stored for a long time.

This was to make a public declaration of his confidence that:

"Fields will be bought for silver, and deeds will be signed, sealed and witnessed in the territory of Benjamin, in the villages around Jerusalem, in the towns of Judah and in the towns of the hill country, of the western foothills and of the Negev, because I will restore their fortunes, declares the Lord" (Jer 32:44).

Jeremiah, of course, was not the only prophet of Israel to base his teaching upon the willingness of God to forgive the sins of his people. Amos was shown a series of judgments that were coming upon the land such as a plague of locusts that would destroy the harvest of the second crop which was traditionally given to the poor people. He was also shown a picture of judgment by fire, but on both occasions when he prayed for forgiveness it was granted and the judgments were withheld. It was only when he saw the Lord standing by a wall with the plumb line that he ceased to ask for forgiveness.

Hosea was another of the prophets who spoke of the forgiveness of God. The whole saga of his marriage was intended to be an illustration of forgiveness in the face of blatant sin and disloyalty. He called upon the people of Israel to return to the Lord asking for forgiveness of their sins in the confidence that God would receive them graciously. In fact, God promised, *"I will heal their waywardness and love them freely, for my anger has turned away from them"* (Hos 14:4).

Blotting out Transgressions

The statement in Isaiah 43:25 *"I, even I, am he who blots out your transgressions for my own sake,"* is hugely significant for an understanding both of the nature of God and of his ways. He does not just forgive sins but he blots them out completely, and he does this not for our sake as miserable sinners, but for his own sake: for his integrity as a God of love and compassion that is equal and opposite to his justice.

Hebraic theology always involves conundrums; it involves dilemma; it poses two opposites and brings them together in tension – creative tension – because most creativity is a product of tension. Just as giving birth to new life involves pain and stress, all human creativity is the product of stress. This is the way God – the God of Creation – has created human beings in his own image, to reflect his creativity, to regenerate life and to fill new wine skins with new wine that would burst old wine skins.

If we are to understand the creative nature of God, we have to grapple with understanding the love and compassion of God, over and against his justice and righteousness. Hosea exactly catches the dilemma at the heart of God in dealing with his sinful people whom he loves with an unbreakable love but cannot embrace because of their sin.

Hosea himself had to go through the terrible experience of his beloved wife deserting him for a life of prostitution from which he had to pay a sum of money to secure her redemption. It was the pain of this experience that enabled him to gain a glimpse of the suffering of God who loved his covenant people so much that he was deeply hurt when they forsook him to worship foreign gods who were nothing but bits of wood and stone.

The Scripture we quoted earlier in this chapter reflects the pain and tension involved in forgiveness: *"My heart is changed within me; all my compassion is aroused. I will not carry out my fierce anger, nor will I turn and devastate Ephraim"* (Hos 8:9-10). In making the decision to forgive and not to punish, God was being true to his own nature, although the price was creative tension – justice demanded punishment, but love called forth forgiveness.

The creative tension of God's love is reflected in Isaiah 54 where God speaks about the time of restoration for the people of Israel whom he is about to release from slavery in Babylon:

"For a brief moment I abandoned you, but with deep compassion I will bring you back. In a surge of anger I hid my face from you for a moment, but with everlasting kindness I will have compassion on you, says the Lord your Redeemer" (Is 54:7).

I remember Eddie Gibbs, who was one of my wife's colleagues in the British Church Growth Association, teaching on this chapter and saying that the great thing about the love of God shown to us in his forgiveness is that his forgiveness is everlasting. It is as though God takes all our sins and dumps them into the deepest ocean and then puts up a notice saying, "NO FISHING!". When God forgives, he does not rake it up at some time later, perhaps when we fall from grace again and we are seeking forgiveness once again. He does not remind us of our previous transgressions because he forgives completely.

The Apostle Paul wonderfully reflects this part of the nature of God in his beautiful love poem in 1 Corinthians 13. He says: *"Love is patient, love is kind. It does not envy, it does not boast, it is not proud. It is not rude, it is not self-seeking, it is not easily angered, it keeps no record of wrongs."* That is the wonderful thing about the love of God – **it keeps no record of wrongs!** This is where so many love relationships, including marriage, become soured – when we say we have forgiven but later we rake it up again when there is another disagreement. True love keeps no record of wrongs! That is the love of God.

A God of Salvation

It was not only forgiveness that was a central part of the nature of God but also there was a desire for *the salvation* of all of humanity. We have already quoted this statement from Ezekiel that God takes no pleasure in the death of the wicked, but rather that they should turn from their wicked ways and live. But Ezekiel made similar statements on other occasions. Both he and Jeremiah spoke of God's willingness to forgive which would lead to the transformation both of individual lives and of the fortunes of the nation.

Jeremiah was told on one occasion to pay a visit to the potter's house as, no doubt, he had done on many occasions. But this time he saw the man trying to make an object that was not possible with that particular piece of clay. But instead of discarding it by throwing it into the dust on his shop-floor, the potter kneaded the clay back into a ball, put it back on the wheel and shaped it into another pot. It was a *different* pot, but it would no doubt have given good service to a busy housewife even though it was not a thing of beauty to decorate the house of a rich person, which was probably the original intention. From this, Jeremiah gained a truth about the nature of God – that he does not discard sinful people but longs for their transformation – for them to recognise their sinfulness and be changed.

Jeremiah received an important message with the possibility of it being applied to the Gentile nations as well as to the covenant people of Israel.

"If at any time, I announce that a nation or kingdom is to be uprooted, torn down and destroyed, and if that nation I warned repents of its evil, then I will relent and not inflict on it the disaster I had planned" (Jer 18:7-8).

This illustrates God's desire to bring salvation to all nations, that he is not only concerned with his covenant people, but with the whole of his creation which includes the Gentile nations.

Ezekiel takes the same principle and applies it to individuals. He says *"if the wicked man turns away from all the sins he has committed and keeps all my decrees and does what is just and right, he will surely live; he will not die"* (Ezek 18:21). But like Jeremiah he also applies this principle to whole nations as in Ezekiel 33:10 where it is applied not just to Judah, but to the whole nation of Israel.

The clearest declarations of God's desire for his message of salvation to be taken to all nations is in Isaiah 49:6 where the prophet was looking forward to the time when the exiles would return to Jerusalem as a redeemed company of believers trusting in their God. He said that the task of restoring the tribes of Jacob and Israel was not the sole purpose of the restoration to the land. But *"I will also make you a light for the Gentiles, that you may bring my salvation to the ends of the earth."*

This was God's ultimate purpose in the Babylonian exile – to cleanse the people of the sin of idolatry and to create a new covenant relationship with them whereby each individual would know God personally and have a faith and trust in him, enabling them to be called *"priests of the Lord . . . ministers of our God"* (Is 61:6).

This new community of believers was fulfilled in New Testament times where they were described by Peter as: *"A chosen people, a royal priesthood, a holy nation, a people belonging to God, that you may declare the praises of him who called you out of darkness into his wonderful light"* (1 Pet 2:9). This was God's desire for his people to be his servants taking the knowledge of his nature and purposes to all peoples and his message of salvation to the world.

CHAPTER FIVE

LISTENING TO GOD

God's most often repeated complaint against his covenant people of Israel through all the writing prophets was that they did not listen to him. Time after time the prophets recorded God's complaint that he had spoken, but nobody had listened. *"All day long I have held out my hands to an obstinate people, who walk in ways not good, pursuing their own imaginations"* (Is 65:2). And later in the same chapter he says *"For I called, but you did not answer, I spoke, but you did not listen. You did evil in my sight and chose what displeases me"* (Is 65:12).

Jeremiah's greatest complaint was that neither the leaders nor the ordinary people listened to the word of God. From the start of his ministry God warned him that the people would fight against him, but that God would strengthen him to resist attacks and give him the strength to deliver unpopular messages. He found, however, that the people not only did not listen when the truth was declared to them, but they did not take any notice of signs that God sent to them. In reporting back to God, he said, *"O Lord, do not your eyes look for truth? You struck them but they felt no pain; you crushed them, but they refused correction. They made their faces harder than stone and refused to repent"* (Jer 5:3).

Warnings Ignored

Jeremiah was no doubt referring to the many natural signs that God had used to send a message to the people, but they had not been heeded. He thought this was because these are only ordinary people; they are uneducated, and they did not know the ways of the Lord. So, he went to the leaders to speak to them with the same negative result. People were just not interested in what God was saying to them. They were perfectly content to work out their own problems and determine their own way of life without divine guidance or interference.

The thing that was far worse in Jeremiah's lifetime was that he perceived the danger on the international front that would have disastrous effects upon the nation but neither the religious leaders nor the political leaders, or indeed the ordinary people, were prepared to face up to the situation and put their trust in God. Instead of this the leaders actually misled the people – this was especially true of the religious leaders who had the responsibility of explaining God's purposes and his requirements to the people. *"They have lied about the Lord; they said, he will do nothing! No harm will come to us; we will never see sword or famine"* (Jer 5:12).

The prophet Amos, more than a hundred years earlier, also had the same complaint. In chapter 4 he lists a series of events that all had spiritual significance with warning messages from God, but nobody took any notice. He said, *"I gave you empty stomachs in every city and a lack of bread in every town, yet you have not returned to me, declares the Lord"* (Am 4:6). He continued with numerous other events that went unheeded: *"Many times I struck your gardens and vineyards, I struck them with blight and mildew. The locusts devoured your fig and olive trees, yet you have not returned to me, declares the Lord"*. The chapter ends with a direct threat of divine judgment.

Of course, Amos knew that all signs need to be interpreted, but he believed God had provided for that. He said, *"Surely the Sovereign Lord does nothing without revealing his plan to his servants the prophets"* (Am 3:7). 800 years later the writer to the Hebrews in the New Testament began with a similar statement. *"In the past God spoke to our forefathers through the prophets at many times and in various ways, but in these last days he has spoken to us by his Son, whom he appointed heir of all things, and through whom he made the universe"* (Heb 1:1-2).

Deeds of the Lord

The prophets of Israel believed that the word of God could be discerned as much from what they called "the deeds of the Lord" as from hearing him speak to them. Often the two were linked; the prophets would see something happen, or hear of a reported event, and God would speak to them concerning its significance.

The Bible declares that the nature of God is unchanging. He is the same yesterday, today and for ever. It was on the basis of this consistency, in contrast to the capricious nature of the Baals, that the prophets were able to declare the word of God with confidence. Elijah, for example, knew that God could answer him on Mount Carmel, whereas the gods of the false prophets were powerless to hear the cries of their devotees (1 Kings 18).

If we deny that God is able to communicate with us today, we deny the unchanging nature of God.

The whole of the Bible declares that God is a God who communicates with the men and women whom he created in his own image, although in every generation, he seeks to communicate in ways that are meaningful in the changing culture and circumstances of that time. There are always some who are able to perceive God's hand in natural events; or see his hand gently guiding the affairs of human beings and speaking to us in different ways. Amos thought that the events he saw in his lifetime were so obvious that everyone ought to have been able to see what God was saying. *"The Sovereign Lord has spoken – who can but prophesy?"* he said. (Am 3:8)

On the other hand, the Apostle Paul discussing the same subject of divine revelation says that God has turned human logic upside down. He says that *"the foolishness of God is wiser than man's wisdom, and the weakness of God is stronger than man's strength"* (1 Cor 1:25). In Paul's understanding God deliberately chose the weak things of the world to shame the strong. *"He chose the lowly things of this world and the despised things – and the things that are not – to nullify the things that are, so that no one may boast before him"* (1 Cor 1:28-29). It was for this reason that Paul did not go to Corinth speaking with great eloquence or superior wisdom, *"but with a demonstration of the Spirit's power, so that your faith might not rest on man's wisdom but on God's power"* (1 Cor 2:4-5).

Communicating Truth

We don't know what demonstration occurred when Paul arrived in Corinth, but all this was leading to his basic declaration about divine revelation and how God speaks to people and reveals his truth to those who are in a close relationship with him. He says *"The man without the Spirit does not accept the things that come from the Spirit of God, for they are foolishness to him, and he cannot understand them, because they are spiritually discerned"* (1 Cor 2:14).

Jesus was confronted with the problem of God's communicating his truth to human beings. The disciples asked him a straight question, *"Why do you speak to the people in parables?"* (Matt 13:10). The answer Jesus gave them was that spiritual discernment had been given to them as his disciples, but to those who did not have the Spirit of God he used homely stories with a heavenly truth. These stories were simple enough for people to understand and discern the deeper meaning behind each story. But Jesus knew that there were some people who would never perceive even the most obvious demonstration of truth. In them there was a blockage against divine truth.

Spiritual Blockage

Jesus referred to what God said to Isaiah at his call to ministry, warning him of what was to come – that whatever he did or said there would be some people who would never accept truth!

"Though seeing, they do not see; though hearing, they do not hear or understand," Jesus said. *"In them is fulfilled the prophecy of Isaiah: you will be ever hearing but never understanding; you will be ever seeing but never perceiving. For this people's heart has become calloused; they hardly hear with their ears and they have closed their eyes. Otherwise they might see with their eyes, hear with their ears, understand with their hearts and turn, and I would heal them"* (Matt 13:13-15).

It is interesting that in Isaiah 6:10-11 which is what Jesus was quoting, there are two different versions with a significant difference. Isaiah 6 records the call to ministry of the young Isaiah in 741 BC, the year King Uzziah died. He had a vision of the glory of God in the temple that led to his call to ministry, hearing the voice of the Lord saying, *"Whom shall I send? And who will go for us?" And I said, "Here am I, send me!" He said, "Go and tell this people: Be ever hearing, but never understanding . . ."*

The Hebrew and Greek texts are quite different. The Hebrew uses the imperative, which implies that God was instructing the prophet to declare the word of God in a way that the people would never understand, they would not perceive the truth that he was declaring.

He was to *"Make the heart of this people calloused; make their ears dull and close their eyes. Otherwise they might see with their eyes, hear with their ears, understand with their hearts and turn and be healed"*.

The Septuagint uses a simple present tense – implying that the hearer will resist the message which is quite different, and according to Matthew it is this Greek text that Jesus quoted – *"You will be ever hearing but never understanding . . ."* This implies that it is the *refusal to believe on the part of the hearers* rather than the deliberate action of the prophet.

Why did Jesus quote from the Greek text rather than the Hebrew? We know that he was fluent in Hebrew because he read from the Hebrew scroll of Isaiah in the synagogue at Nazareth, much to the astonishment of the congregation (Luke 4:22). Jesus, of course, would have known that the prophets made no distinction between the direct and the indirect will of God – between the things that God actually did, and the things that he allowed to happen. It was all the same to the prophets: they were all the deeds of the Lord.

It may be that Jesus, knowing that his teaching would go out into the Gentile world long after his earthly ministry ended, used the Greek translation which he knew would be more acceptable in western culture. But in practice, Jesus knew that there is something in our human nature that acts as a blockage to truth when we have been exposed to the sinfulness of human nature for a long time. This was evidently the situation with Nicodemus, a senior rabbi, who secretly came to see Jesus and was told that he had to be born again in order to see the kingdom of God.

Jesus no doubt knew that the years of rabbinical training Nicodemus had received had created a type of institutional blockage that did not allow for any revelation of divine truth that was outside his intellectual system. A similar problem exists today with the majority of clergy and ministers in the denominational churches whose academic training (like my own) has been dominated by sterile biblical criticism and liberal theology, that robs the student of a personal faith in a living and active God – the God of Abraham, Isaac and Jacob, the Creator of the Universe.

Interpreting Signs Today

This is the tragedy we face today; the vast majority of human beings in Western nations such as Britain are so steeped in the culture of secular humanism that they are impervious to spiritual truth. We are forewarned of this in 2 Timothy 4:3-4, *"For the time will come when men will not put up with sound doctrine. Instead, to suit their own desires, they will gather around them a number of teachers to say what their itching ears want to hear. They will turn their ears away from the truth and turn aside to myths."*

This is the kind of popular teaching that is being fed to the public today by rabid evolutionary and population-control gurus, such as Chris Packham, the popular wildlife presenter on BBC television who said in April 2020 "NOTHING but humans are going to save the world!" He said, "Nothing from beyond our world can save the planet", while popular cosmologist Lawrence Krauss went even further, saying "The stars are going to save us – NOT JESUS!"

Sadly, millions listen to the rants of these ignorant Darwinian gurus who have the ear of the public. They are ignorant because they have no understanding of truth and what is even worse – they have no awareness of their ignorance! They are especially influential with young people who are concerned about the state of the environment and who live in a world of social media dominated by secularists who fill them with horror stories of the destruction of the rainforests and the pollution of the oceans and the air we breathe. But they fail to perceive the even more fundamental pollution of the moral and spiritual arteries of humanity that are driving the world towards far greater calamities than those which are engulfing the physical environment.

What Paul was foreseeing in his advice to Timothy was about the general trends in society, but Peter looks beyond the secular leaders to the religious leaders, noting that among church leaders there would be false prophets and teachers. He says:

"But there were also false prophets among the people, just as there will be false teachers among you. They will secretly introduce destructive heresies, even denying the Sovereign Lord who bought them – bringing swift destruction on themselves." He adds, *"Many will follow their shameful ways and will bring the way of truth into disrepute"* (2 Pet 2:1-2).

The fundamental problem we have today is that we not only have the popular media dominated by secularists who have the ear of the majority of the population in Western nations, but those who should be able to interpret the word of God to the biblically illiterate population are blinded by unbelief. We have a generation of church leaders in positions of power in the denominations who have been trained in academic institutions that have a long tradition of biblical liberalism and replacement theology.

It is this combination that undermines faith in the God of Creation who spoke to the patriarchs and the prophets of Israel, and who revealed his unchanging nature and laid the foundation for the coming of Messiah Jesus. Without that foundation rooted in the history of God's dealings with his covenant people we are stripped of an essential understanding of what God is doing today and what we should be declaring to the secular authorities in the nations.

If church leaders and theologians do not understand the nature and purposes of God revealed in the deeds of the Lord and the history of his relationship with the people of Israel, they will be powerless to interpret the signs of the times in which we are living today. The command of Jesus to his followers to 'watch and pray' was intended to be accompanied by the ability to interpret the spiritual significance of everyday events that perplex the population or are dismissed with rational explanations by secular humanists.

Signs of Disaster in the 1980s

God has been sending us a succession of signs long before the outbreak of the coronavirus pandemic, and they continue today. By way of illustration we can look at the 1980s when there were a number of disasters which had some spiritual significance. In the old printed magazine *Prophecy Today*, we noted these and offered an interpretation to each of them, but most church leaders simply ignored them. The most notorious event was the first of the series. It was specifically directed to the church.

York Minster

On the night of the 9th July 1984 there was a serious fire at York Minster where only hours before David Jenkins had been installed as Bishop of Durham. He was one of the most outspoken of the liberal theologians. He once described the Resurrection as 'a conjuring trick with bones'. He openly declared many of the miracles in the New Testament as myths and folk tales and he dismissed the Virgin Birth and many other tenets of the Christian faith as unbelievable.

Even the secular press could see the link between the York Minster fire and the consecration of David Jenkins – it was so obvious that this was divine judgment on unbelief that it was difficult to dismiss. But that was precisely what the Archbishop of Canterbury did. The fire had been caused by a lightning strike that was so powerful it overrode a newly installed lightning conductor system designed to protect the building. It was even more remarkable because there was one tiny cloud in an otherwise clear night sky that came across to York and released this massive lightning strike directly onto the Minster out of a virtually cloudless sky.

I remember listening to Archbishop Robert Runcie being interviewed on the 1 o'clock news on the day of the fire, when the reporter said that this had to be a message from God. The Archbishop vehemently denied this, saying that God does not do things like that, and that God is not in direct control of the weather. It emerged later that if the Archbishop had admitted it to be an 'act of God' the insurance on the newly installed lightning conductor might have been null and void, so the Archbishop was under the pressures of Mammon in defending his liberal theology.

Bradford City

The fact that senior church leaders could not even interpret a sign on one of their own buildings set the example for dealing with the series of signs that followed through the 1980s. The next one was also in Yorkshire. On 11 May 1985 a stand full of football fans, caught fire at the Bradford City football ground during a match which left 56 people dead. The fire that afternoon followed a morning ceremony in the City Hall where Britain's first Muslim Mayor had been installed, taking office through swearing allegiance on the Qur'an.

The first sign had been about unbelief in the church and the second was about allowing other religions to establish spiritual strongholds in the nation in denial of the centuries of Judeo-Christian heritage of Britain.

'Herald of Free Enterprise'

The next sign came on 6 March 1987 with the capsizing of the *'Herald of Free Enterprise'*, a car and passenger ferry that had just left Zeebrugge on a journey to Dover. There was a loss of nearly 200 lives. It was caused by human error as it left the harbour with its bow doors open. The man responsible for closing these doors was asleep in his cabin. There were a number of messages here about being watchful, but there was clearly something wrong in the procedures of this shipping line that was intent on maximising profit by rapid turnaround on their journeys across the channel. When making money becomes more important than human safety there is clearly something wrong in a system driven by greed.

Hungerford

The next disaster was in the sleepy little town of Hungerford where there was a massacre in which a young man driven by satanic possession, believing he was serving a serpent god who spoke messages to him, went on a rampage of murder and mayhem through the quiet country town killing people at random with an automatic weapon. This was a clear warning about the dangers of occultism, violence and murder.

Hurricane

The next sign was the great storm with hurricane force winds that swept across south-east England, the wealthiest area in the country on the night of Friday 16 October 1987. The force of the wind destroyed 16 million trees in two hours of mayhem. It destroyed the entire harvest of fruit in the apple orchards of Kent, known as the garden of England, and it caused enormous damage to houses and cars, and other properties valued at more than half £1 billion.

Hurricane Friday was followed by Black Monday in the City of London as winds of panic swept through the financial markets wiping millions of dollars off stocks and shares across the world as other financial institutions followed suit. This was yet another sign of greed and corruption in the financial systems of the world with its vast inequalities that condemns two thirds of the world's population to live in poverty and a tiny minority who exercise a controlling interest and indulge in unseemly wealth.

King's Cross Fire

The hurricane and the stock market crash were followed just one month later by a disastrous fire in King's Cross underground station on 18 November 1987 in which 31 people died and 100 were injured, many of them seriously. The fire started in accumulated rubbish underneath a wooden escalator serving the Victoria line. It was thought to have been started accidentally by someone dropping a lighted match as they were about to board the escalator to exit the station. It triggered a firestorm that swept up the escalator into the ticket hall killing all those still in the hall. But there had been several reports about the danger of rubbish underneath the wooden escalator that had been ignored which was a clear message about ignoring warnings.

Midlands Airport

The Kings Cross disaster was followed a few weeks later, on 9 January 1989, by the crash of a passenger aircraft attempting to land at the Midlands Airport and falling short onto the M1 motorway. This was caused by confusion in the cockpit between the pilot and co-pilot who were arguing when a fault in one engine occurred and the pilot closed down the good engine rather than the one that had developed a fault. So they lost power in both engines and fell short of the runway. Disunity and confusion in a leadership team can have fatal consequences.

Hillsborough

Three months later, on 15 April 1989, the disastrous Hillsborough football tragedy occurred in which 96 people lost their lives. The enquiry into this incident rumbled on for another 30 years – the intensity of the passions evoked by this accident caused by overcrowding and panic were unbearable for many of the families who lost loved ones, especially children. Our involvement as a Ministry was that a year previously our Ministry Team had been doing a week's ministry in Sheffield at the end of which one of the team, the Rev Edmund Heddle, had a vivid revelation of the accident as we drove past the football ground on the way to the final meeting. He described in detail many adults and children being crushed to death which he repeated to the 80 clergy and church leaders present, urging them to contact the football authorities warning them of danger. But none of them took this warning seriously so they failed to contact the football club. A number of the clergy wrote to us afterwards bitterly regretting that they had ignored the warning.

'Marchioness'

This was followed on 20 August 1989 by the sinking of the 'Marchioness' on the River Thames in London with the loss of 51 lives. It was caused by the collision of the pleasure boat, celebrating a birthday event, with a dredger – both were moving in the same direction downstream, but neither vessel had a lookout on watch. Clearly, the spiritual sign was the lack of watchfulness.

AIDS

The final sign of the 1980s was the outbreak of AIDS that began during the decade and has since been responsible for the death of many millions across the world. It was mainly found among homosexual men and as a sign it carried a clear warning about the physical dangers of misusing the natural practice of sexual love; and the spiritual sin of lust, which Paul describes in Romans 1:27 as, *"Men committed indecent acts with other men, and received in themselves the due penalty for their perversion"*. The spiritual sign was masked by the publication of a government circular on 'Safe Sex' which urged the public to use a condom when engaging in sexual intercourse. There were no warnings from either church or state about casual sex of any kind, and there was no moral content to the government paper – just a health warning.

Interpreting the Signs

The deeds of the Lord need interpretation, and this is the prophetic task of the church among whose leaders there should be men and women in each nation with the ability to understand the spiritual significance of events that are taking place in the life of that nation. In biblical language these are 'signs'– an event in the world of nature, or of human origin, that can convey a spiritual message.

The 1980s, although being the height of the Charismatic Movement, did not produce leaders with the ability to bring the word of God to the nation. The movement achieved nothing to halt the downward trend in the influence of the institutional churches in the life of the British nation. Certainly, there was no spiritual revival which was much heralded in prophecies given at multitudes of meetings organised by churches and charismatic ministries in that decade.

This failure to influence the nation is largely because the charismatic renewal movement concentrated attention upon celebrating the spiritual gifts of the New Testament, while neglecting to preach the whole word of God in the Bible. So people were not given an understanding of the 'deeds of the Lord' through which God speaks to the nations. Church leaders failed to teach the people that the spiritual gifts are given to equip the people of God to fulfil the 'Great Commission' and not to entertain the people. So, the people were not taught to discern the deeds of the Lord and to interpret the word of God to those who do not know him.

Discerning Signs

The first sign in the Bible is one of beauty and mercy. After the evil generation of Noah's day had been destroyed, God began again with Noah and his family. As they emerged from the Ark to begin a new life, God showed them a beautiful sign and said, *"I have set my rainbow in the clouds"*. It was not left to a prophet to explain its meaning, for God himself revealed its significance when he said, *"This is the sign of the covenant I am making between me and you and every living creature"* (Gen 9:12).

Jesus spoke about discerning the spiritual significance of signs, both in the world of nature and of human activity. In Luke's gospel 12:54 we read *"He said to the crowd: when you see a cloud rising in the west, immediately you say, 'It's going to rain', and it does. And when the south wind blows, you say, 'It's going to be hot', and it is. Hypocrites! You know how to interpret the appearance of the earth and the sky. How is it that you don't know how to interpret this present time?"*

2000 years later God is saying exactly the same thing to this present generation. In his lifetime Jesus was speaking to the ordinary people in the street who were looking for a Messiah. But the true message of the prophets about the forthcoming Messiah had been corrupted by the false teaching of the scribes and Pharisees. A similar thing happened in Jeremiah's day with terrible consequences for his generation. In the lifetime of Jesus the people did not know the word of God sufficiently well to be able to discern the *Logos*[5] who had come as *"a light shining in the darkness"* to make his dwelling among them. So, when given the choice, they chose a robber and crucified the Son of Righteousness, who had been dwelling in their midst.

The Words of Jesus

Jesus went on to explain another contemporary sign that the people had misunderstood. Pilate had carried out some atrocity in Galilee that everyone was talking about; but Jesus used the event to give a warning that this was a sign of what would happen in the near future. He said that they could foretell the weather, but they could not interpret spiritual signs. Unless there was repentance and turning in the nation, they would all suffer. He added:

"Or those eighteen who died when the tower of Siloam fell on them – do you think they were more guilty than all the others living in Jerusalem? I tell you, no! But unless you repent, you too will all perish" (Luke 13:4).

The words of Jesus were fearfully fulfilled in the lifetime of many of those who heard him speak when the revolution in Judaea against

---

5 This Greek expression meaning 'reason' or 'word', is used in the prologue to John's Gospel, John 1:1.

the Romans broke out in 66 AD, just over 30 years after the ministry of Jesus, and half a million people were slaughtered in the region, and once again Jerusalem was destroyed. When God pronounces a warning there is a terrible finality about the consequences of refusing to heed the warning.

Desolations

This is what lay behind the writing of the Psalmist in Psalm 46 where he begins by saying that *"God is our refuge and strength, an ever present help in trouble"* which are words of comfort that have strengthened the faith of countless millions of believers over the years. It was certainly one of the favourite Bible passages that was read in my family when we sat in the air raid shelter in London during the Second World War listening to the bombs falling around us and feeling the ground shake beneath our feet as a stick of bombs came closer. My sister and I snuggled closer to my mother who constantly read the Bible to us with Psalms such as 46 and 91 and many of the words of Jesus.

But the Psalmist does not only say nice comforting things, he invites us to come with him to see *"The works of the Lord, the desolations he has brought on earth"* (Ps 46:8). I can remember in the later days of World War II when the flying bombs were dropping out of the sky. I was a teenager by then and I was caught away from home during an air raid when I sought refuge in an underground shelter in London. I was blown off my feet and I staggered out into the daylight to see a scene of utter desolation with human bodies blown to pieces. A bomb had hit a street shelter. As a child it scarred my memory for life and was a scene that has never left me as it is too horrible to describe. I have asked myself this many times – did God do that? Of course not! But undoubtedly, he allowed it to happen as part of the wickedness of our unredeemed humanity. He allows such things after the warnings he has sent time after time have all been ignored. We ***must*** understand the nature of God – ***his justice*** as well as his love, if we are rightly to interpret the signs that are all around us today.

The Desolation of Judah

God did not stop the Babylonians from breaking down the walls of Jerusalem and carrying out the most fearful destruction; slaughtering the people mercilessly, raping the women in the King's family in front of him; then killing his sons and other male relatives, and finally gouging out his eyes and taking him blind as a captive of war to be paraded through the streets of Babylon.

Was it God's will that this should happen? – Undoubtedly not! But God knew it would happen unless there was repentance in Jerusalem, and he revealed the tragedy to Jeremiah ahead of time, so that he could warn the King personally and all the people. Jeremiah said to King Zedekiah,

"This is what the Lord God Almighty, the God of Israel says: if you surrender to the officers of the king of Babylon, your life will be spared and this city will not be burned down; you and your family will live. But if you will not surrender to the officers of the king of Babylon, this city will be handed over to the Babylonians and they will burn it down; you yourself will not escape from their hands" (Jer 38:17-18).

The warning could not have been clearer; but it was ignored with tragic consequences.

Jeremiah's Warnings

I have lived with the prophet Jeremiah for the past 40 years, studying his writings, reliving some of his experiences and trying to get into an understanding of his mind and heart. I share, to some extent, the pain he felt when his words of warning went unheeded, *"Oh, that my head were a spring of water and my eyes a fountain of tears! I would weep day and night for the slain of my people"* (Jer 9:1). This was long before the actual destruction of Jerusalem. He was already foreseeing the terrible events that lay ahead and despite all the warnings that he gave, his words were ignored. I still cannot read Jeremiah 52 without experiencing a terrible sense of dread.

I have benefited in so many ways from learning how Jeremiah was able to stand in the Council of the Lord, and how he was always alert for anything that the Lord would use to convey a message to him.

My own experience, of course, is in no way to be compared with Jeremiah's, but I have spent the last 40 years bringing warnings that have been ignored. My first book of warning was *Towards the Dawn*.[6] It was a very different world then. But the secularisation of Britain had begun 20 years earlier and was now beginning to show clear signs of corruption in society, especially through the breakdown of family and marriage.

1980 was the first year since records began that babies born out of wedlock in Britain exceeded 10%. But already I was looking at the trends and foreseeing the path ahead; and giving warnings. My next book followed just two years later. It was *The Day Comes*, with a Foreword by one of the leading evangelical academics of the day, F.F. Bruce.[7] It was full of warnings of things to come – some of which have already happened.

I can, at least, say that I share some of the sadness and deep concerns that Jeremiah experienced when his words of warning were not heeded. I too have a great love for my country and my countrymen and women, and like Jeremiah, I know that if there is not repentance and turning, tragedy and suffering lie ahead.

In the next two chapters we will review some of the path we have trodden as a nation to get to this present situation. It is always necessary when we reach a critical point in our national history to retrace steps in order to understand the situation clearly, before attempting to offer any suggestions for the way ahead.

---

6 Clifford Hill, *Towards the Dawn*, Collins, London 1980.

7 Clifford Hill, *The Day Comes – a Prophetic View of the Contemporary World*, Collins, London 1982.

CHAPTER 6

THE GOD WHO LOVES US AND
SPEAKS TO US

God has never left himself without a witness in every generation.
He seeks ways to communicate with those who are open to listen to
him and to receive his love and direction in their lives. Not all the
words of the prophets were words of warning or rebuke. The Prophet
Isaiah received a word of comfort during a troubled time in Jerusalem
in the eighth century BC. He said:

*"O people of Zion, who live in Jerusalem, you will weep no more.
How gracious he will be when you cry for help! As soon as he hears, he
will answer you. Although the Lord gives you the bread of adversity and
the water of affliction . . . Whether you turn to the right or to the left,
your ears will hear a voice behind you, saying, 'This is the way; walk in
it'"* (Is 30:19-21).

God has many times spoken to us, his people in Britain; to any
who are open to hear from him. He has spoken in many and various
ways to many people. In times past – especially in days of great
turmoil during the Second World War, God has spoken to those with
ears to hear. But it was the Charismatic Movement in the 1970s and
80s that popularised prophecy, particularly in the New Churches and
the Pentecostal denominations.

There was not a lot of biblical teaching on the subject of
prophecy in those days and sometimes prophecy slipped through into
church fellowships on the back of the gift of tongues when it was not
rigorously weighed. When prophecies are given in the name of God
and subsequently prove to be untrue, they have a seriously damaging
effect upon the whole church.

False Teaching

When these prophecies are repeated year after year and developed in various forms, as 'The Latter Rain' prophecies have been which have influenced the course of the Charismatic Movement, they should be examined for biblical accuracy and if found to be in error they should be declared anathema in the church. In this regard the greatest weakness of the charismatic churches has been the tendency to formulate doctrine on the basis of contemporary revelation, rather than on the basis of Scripture.

Sadly, a lot of this false teaching has got into churches of all denominations, especially through the lyrics of worship songs. The prime example is the New Apostolic Reformation Movement (NAR) where teaching comes directly from the Latter Rain heresies dating back to the 1940s but is still embraced by some churches today.

In the 1970s and 80s, an increasing number of mainline churches as well as the new churches were becoming involved in the Charismatic Movement, if only through the use of new songs in their worship. But prophecy was one of the gifts of the Spirit that were increasingly being heard in charismatic meetings and in worship services. It was in response to this that Prophetic Word Ministries (PWM) began publishing in *Prophecy Today* magazine a series of teaching articles on biblical prophecy to help people to discern false prophecy.

By far the most popular prophecies among charismatics in those days were promises of revival, great power and prosperity. These were all based upon the belief in a great 'end time harvest' for the kingdom before the second coming of Christ, which is the exact opposite of the teaching of Jesus in Matthew 24 where he said that believers will experience persecution and not great popularity. These popular prophecies pre-dated the Charismatic Movement and had their origin in the Latter Rain revival movement in North America. But they were widely believed, and their influence is still to be seen today.

False Prophecy

In the 1980s the drift away from biblical truth and the embracing of lies under the guise of popular prophecy became widespread, through the Charismatic Movement that was reaching into churches of all denominations. An example of the harm being done by false prophecy is seen in a prophecy given by David Minor to an assembly of the Lutheran Church in the USA in 1988 which was widely circulated right across the Western nations and became very popular in Britain even in traditional evangelical churches. It conveyed a promise of revival preceded by a time of cleansing in the church. These were described as 'winds'. It is a long prophecy, but it is necessary to produce it here to illustrate the extent of the deception that ran through, not only the New Churches, but through the mainline denominations in the 1980s. It was entitled:

TURN YOUR FACE INTO THE WIND

'The Spirit of God would say to you that the Wind of the Holy Spirit is blowing through the land. The church, however, is incapable of fully recognising this Wind. Just as your nation has given names to its hurricanes, so I have put my Name on this Wind. This Wind shall be named "Holiness unto the Lord".

'Because of the lack of understanding, some of my people will try to find shelter from the wind, but in so doing they shall miss my work. For this wind has been sent to blow through every institution that has been raised in my name. Those institutions that have substituted their name for mine, they shall fall by the impact of My Wind. Those institutions shall fall like cardboard shacks in a gale. Ministries that have not walked in uprightness before me shall be broken and fall.

'For this reason, man will be tempted to brand this as the work of Satan, but do not be misled. This is My Wind, I cannot tolerate my church in its present form, nor will I tolerate it. Ministries and organisations will shake and fall in the face of this Wind, and even though some will seek to hide from that Wind, they shall not escape, it shall blow against your lives and all around you will appear crumbling. And so it shall.

'But never forget this is My Wind, saith the Lord, with tornado force it will come and appear to leave devastation, but the Word of the Lord comes and says, "Turn your face into the Wind and let it blow." For only that which is not of me shall be devastated. You must see this as necessary.

'Be not dismayed. For after this, My Wind shall blow again. Have you not read how My Breath blew on the valley of dry bones? So it shall breathe on you. This Wind will come in equal force as the first Wind. This Wind too will have a name. It shall be called "The Kingdom of God".

'It shall bring My government and order. Along with that it shall bring My power. The supernatural shall come in that wind. The world will laugh at you because of the devastation of that first wind, but they will laugh no more. For this Wind will come with force and power that will produce the miraculous among my people and the fear of God shall fall on the nation.

'My people will be willing in the day of My power, saith the Lord. In my first Wind that is upon you now, I will blow out pride, lust, greed, competition and jealousy, and you will feel devastated. But haven't you read, "Blessed are the poor in spirit, for theirs is the Kingdom of Heaven"? So out of your poverty of spirit I will establish my Kingdom. Have you not read, "The Kingdom of God is in the Holy Ghost?" So, by my Spirit, my Kingdom will be established and made manifest.

'Know this also, there will be those who shall seek to hide from this present Wind and they will try to flow with the second Wind. But again, they will be blown away by it. Only those who have turned their faces into the present Wind shall be allowed to be propelled by the second Wind.

'You have longed for revival and a return of the miraculous and the supernatural. You and your generation shall see it, but it shall only come by my process, saith the Lord. The church of this nation cannot contain my power in its present form. But as it turns to the Wind of the Holiness of God, it shall be purged and changed to contain my glory. This is judgment that has begun at the house of God, but it is not the end. When the second Wind has come and brought in my harvest, then shall the end come.'[8]

This prophecy was widely circulated among churches of all types and denominations as a true word from God and it became highly influential in charismatic circles. **But it was untrue, even though it included phrases that in the right context would be true. These references deceived many people and made the utterance a false prophecy which did great harm.** But the very fact that it was accepted

---

8 I have used this prophecy in chapter 5, 'The role of prophecy in the direction of the charismatic movement' in Clifford Hill, Peter Fenwick, David Forbes, David Noakes, *Blessing the Church?,* Eagle Publishers, Guildford, 1995, page 122.

uncritically shows the biblical poverty of the churches. Even a simple knowledge of the Bible should have enabled people to see through this piece of deception, given as coming from the mouth of God.

Evaluation

There was plenty of evidence of "pride, lust, greed, competition and jealousy" in the churches and among church leaders which no doubt made the word seem acceptable. But why should people "feel devastated" when the wind blew those things away? Calling this wind "Holiness unto the Lord" was certainly not in accordance with the biblical concept of 'holiness' as separation from the world.

If the writer had actually studied Ezekiel and not just read the vision of the 'valley of dry bones' he would have understood 'holiness' as Moses and the prophets used the term. Where does the Bible say "The Kingdom of God is the Holy Ghost"? And the declaration, "By My Spirit, my Kingdom will be established and made manifest" is in that context pure 'Latter Rain Manifest Sons of God' drivel.

Then, 'The Second Wind' is slipped into the mix with the promise of a revival and supernatural power available to believers. This is exactly the popular heresy promoted by Latter Rain proponents since the 1940s. Of course, there was nothing more appealing to church leaders and worldly Christians of the 80s and 90s than the promise of divine power as they watched their congregations dwindle and felt powerless. Sadly, these false promises still hang around today in churches that cling onto NAR concepts and allow them into their worship songs.

There were many more prophecies making expansive promises of both social and spiritual power coming to Christians that excited many people at the height of the Charismatic Movement in the 1980s that greatly concerned us. There had been very little teaching about prophecy in churches of any denominations, and from the 1960s onwards there was a drift away from exegetical preaching. Study of the Old Testament was neglected and not even read in many churches. The whole word of God was rarely heard which opened the way for deception and false prophecy. The Charismatic Movement became increasingly separated from sound biblical scholarship as it became driven by the values of pragmatism – anything that attracted people and drew the crowds was embraced.

It was due to our desire to promote greater understanding of biblical prophecy that we began publishing the magazine *Prophecy Today* in 1985. That objective is still with us in publishing the online version *Prophecy Today UK*, which since 2015 has been a weekly magazine publishing a fresh issue every Friday, with a biblically based comment on current affairs and a range of other articles. When we began publishing the printed magazine *Prophecy Today* people began sending prophetic words to us. This made it all the more urgent to establish biblical standards of truth for judging prophecy.

Defining True Prophecy

Modern prophecy does not carry the authority of Scripture, although the Bible sets the standard of truth whereby any modern words purporting to have come from God must be tested. All genuine words have to go through human minds which inevitably affects the way the thoughts are expressed. Human beings who are in a close relationship with God through faithful devotion, intercession and study of the Bible, may receive thoughts which they express in their own words which reflect something of what God is conveying to us today.

Prophecy Today Publications

A small selection of the many words received in the 1980s and 90s are reproduced below. They were all deemed to have sufficient biblical truth to be worthy of publication. We recognised that no modern prophecy is word for word directly from God: and no contemporary words are on the level of biblical prophecy. Those who are seeking truth, and are attempting to listen to the Lord, express in their own words what they are hearing. This must be carefully weighed and considered in the context of biblical truth as defining the standard of biblical revelation. The selection below were words sent to us by readers, or from trusted Christian leaders: each went through our weighing and testing process and were judged to have a sufficient element of truth to be offered to the public.

The first we published was given by Shirley Archer in Tunbridge Wells Christian Fellowship in November 1984. This was given at a time when the Charismatic Movement was at its height in Britain and Christians were ignoring the rapid social changes that were taking place in the nation. It was a call for greater vigilance, prayer and repentance. It was specifically addressed to Christians.

SOUND THE TRUMPET

November 1984

'My children consider well your nation. Look around you, observe your homes, schools, business and institutions of law and government.

'What do you see? Do you see the violence, the corruption, the rebellion and the anarchy? Do you see the anguish and suffering of the victims of such evil?

'Do you see the anguish of your God? For I weep and grieve deeply over a nation that once honoured my name and respected my word; a nation that was once great but is now grovelling in the dust. But I say to you even now, all is not lost.

'Even though my righteousness demands that I severely judge the wickedness of this people, yet in mercy I wait. I wait for my people to come before me with weeping, fasting and prayer. I wait for intercessors who will continue to stand in the gap and hold back my hand of judgment, so I can continue to pour out my Spirit on this land.

'But I warn you, in great earnestness, that I will not wait much longer. For although my Spirit is even now moving in great power through this land, Satan is also active, deceiving and lulling my people into a false peace of complacency and security, causing them to sleep instead of being alert to watch, and pray.

'So I would have you sound the trumpet; calling my people to earnest, continuous prayer, so that I can fulfil my desire to pour blessings on this nation, rather than judgments.

'Then once more, it will be said of this land: "Blessed is the nation whose God is the Lord."'

The 1980s was a time of great hope among Christians, many of whom were greatly excited by the new enthusiasm and signs of fresh spiritual life in denominational churches that had been stuck in a rut of tradition for a long time. The next word was clearly addressed to such a situation. It was a word that I received during a meeting of the trustees of Prophetic Word Ministries (PWM) in May 1985.

IF MY PEOPLE

May 1985

Thus says the Lord to the Christians of the West, 'I am longing to bring revival to you. I am longing to save the nations of the West whom I love. But the forces of corruption are already far advanced. They are eating like a cancer into the bodies of the nations. They are draining the life from the body, sapping the power to resist the destructive forces of the enemy.

'There will be no revival among the nations of the West until my people turn to me in true repentance. If my people who are called by my name will heed my word and turn from their faithless ways and come weeping before me with tears of true repentance then I will hear their prayer, for I love them, and I will pour out my Spirit upon them and heal their lands.'

A word of warning was given in January 1986 that called for a spirit of repentance in the churches. It was given by Roger Jamieson, a church leader in Marlow, Buckinghamshire. It was one of many of a similar nature addressed to the churches in Britain.

A WORD OF WARNING

January 1986

'The times are urgent, my children, and you are not sufficiently aware of the pressing need calling for repentance and speaking into situations in the power of the Holy Spirit to proclaim my name. The spirit of the antichrist is moving among the nations and is in your nation.

'Unless you repent, all that is from the past will happen again but with severer form and yet more horror. This is because my people will not listen nor will they discern the times.

'Seek my Face, seek my Spirit and know that I would give you words to utter, but you must pay the cost of commitment out of love. Trust me for I will enable you to do all things that I require so that my judgments may be turned just as they were at Nineveh when the king and the people repented at the preaching of Jonah.'

The next is a significant word from David Noakes given at a PWM public meeting in March 1986. Once again, the background was the widespread expectation among Christians of a great harvest for the gospel as the Charismatic Movement reached its height in drawing large numbers of people to meetings where exciting things were happening.

Some of the things that were happening were clearly not of the Holy Spirit and were engendering false hopes among the people. This was because the message being proclaimed was ignoring the spiritual and moral state of the nation, so it was not a true gospel calling for repentance, and this is the relevance of this word of warning brought by David.

TIMES OF REFRESHING

March 1986

God is saying to us, 'I desire to restrain the darkness so that even though there is much shaking, nevertheless it will remain possible for my people to do the works of God and to bring in a great harvest through evangelism. I want my people to pray that I will restrain the darkness for this purpose. I desire to extend the time of grace during which it remains light, and in mercy to limit the shaking to that which will accomplish my purpose of causing men to despair of themselves and to turn to me for salvation.

'If my people will pray in this way, and if they are willing to repent and to do the works of God wholeheartedly while it remains possible to do so, then I will indeed restrain the darkness and maintain the conditions of light in which my work can be done.

'Cry to me to maintain the light, cry to me to send labourers into the harvest, and consecrate yourselves to be a holy people to carry out the Great Commission of evangelism in this lost world. If you will do this, then I will hear from heaven and send times of refreshing to you, for I desire revival rather than judgment.

'What I will do depends on the response of my own people, who are called by my name. If you will hear my call, then I also will be faithful to respond in this way; but if your ears remain closed, then surely, I will allow the times of darkness to come upon you quickly. This is the hour of decision and I place the choice before you.'

The following month, April 1986, the much anticipated gathering of men and women with prophetic ministries at Mount Carmel in Israel took place. It was linked with a week-long gathering of 5000 people from all over the world in Jerusalem. This was a conference with seminars and evening celebration meetings which gave opportunity for those who had been at Carmel to report on what they were hearing from the Lord.

After a 24 hour period of silence seeking God in prayer there was unanimity in affirming that the major words that we were hearing were from Haggai 2 and Hebrews 12 where God was declaring that the day would come when he would SHAKE the whole world of nature and all nations. The following word of prophecy was given to Lance Lambert, a Jewish Messianic leader residing in Jerusalem. This prophecy has been widely circulated around the world, and among discerning Christians it is considered to be one of the most authentic words from God received in recent times.

This is the word as Lance received it:

SHAKING THE NATIONS

April 1986

'It will not be long before there will come upon the world a time of unparalleled upheaval and turmoil. Do not fear for it is I the Lord who am shaking all things. I began this shaking with the First World War and I greatly increased it through the Second World War. Since 1973 I have given it an even greater impetus. In the last stage I plan to complete it with the shaking of the universe itself, with signs in the sun and moon and stars. But before that point is reached, I will judge the nations, and the time is near. It will not only be by war and civil war, by anarchy and terrorism, and by monetary collapses that I will judge the nations, but also by natural disasters; by earthquakes, by shortages and famines, and by old and new plague diseases. I will also judge them by giving them over to their own ways, to lawlessness, to loveless selfishness, to delusion and to believing a lie, to false religion and an apostate church, even to a Christianity without me.

'Do not fear when these things begin to happen, for I disclose these things to you before they commence in order that you might be prepared, and that in the day of trouble and of evil you may stand firm and overcome. For I purpose that you may become the means of encouraging and strengthening many who love me but who are weak. I desire that through you many may become strong in me, and that multitudes of others might find my salvation through you.

'And hear this! Do not fear the power of the Kremlin, nor the power of the Islamic revolution, for I plan to break both of them through Israel. I will bring down their pride and their arrogance, and shatter them because they have blasphemed my name. In that day I will avenge the blood of all the martyrs and the innocent ones whom they have slaughtered. I will surely do this thing for they have thought that there was no one to judge them. But I have seen their ways and I have heard the cries of the oppressed and of the persecuted and I will break their power and make an end of them. Be prepared therefore for when all this comes to pass; to you will be given the last great opportunity to preach the gospel freely to all the nations.

'In the midst of all the turmoil and shaking, and at the heart of everything is my church. In the heavenlies she is joined to me in one Spirit and I have destined her for the throne. You who are my beloved whom I have redeemed and anointed – you are mine. I will equip and empower you and you will rise up and do great things in my name, even in the midst of darkness and evil. For I will reveal my power and my grace and my Glory through you. Do not hold back or question my ways with you for in all my dealings with you I have always had in mind that you should be part of my bride and reign with me. Do not forget that this requires a special discipline and training. So yield to me that I might do a work in you in the time which is left for I plan even during this shaking that the bride will make herself ready.

'And in the midst of nations on earth seething with unrest and conflict, I have set my Israel. Yes, I say **MY** Israel, even though they walk in disobedience and transgression, in the stubbornness of their hearts, divorced from me through unbelief. Nevertheless, always remember that I made them enemies of the gospel for your sake. I the Lord, I myself blinded them and hardened them that salvation might come to the Gentiles in fulness. Yet they are still mine, beloved of me with a tender and an undying love. They are my kith and kin and I love them. Shall I give them up for all that they have done to me, says the Lord? Yet I have surrendered them to sorrow, to anguish of heart and to continual suffering. But I have never given them up. In all their affliction I was afflicted though I neither delivered nor saved them from death. Nevertheless, I have been present, I, the King of Israel, I have been present, although unnoticed and unregarded, in all their sufferings. There was no gas chamber, no massacre in which I was not present. But now the time has surely come when I shall receive them, for I will reveal myself to them and with astonishment they will recognise me.

'For in the midst of these judgments multitudes upon multitudes will be saved from the nations. You will hardly know how to bring the harvest in, but my Spirit will equip you for the task. And to Israel will I turn in that day, and I will melt the hardening which has befallen her. I will turn her blindness into clear sight, and tear away the veil on her heart. Then shall she be redeemed with heart bursting joy, and will become a fountain of new and resurrection life to the whole company of the redeemed.

'Do not fear for these days, for I have purposed that you should stand with me and serve me in them. Fear not, for I love you and I will protect you and equip you. I, the Lord, will anoint you with a new anointing and you will work my works and fulfil my counsel. You shall stand before me, the Lord of the whole earth, and serve me with understanding and with power, and you shall reign with me during those days. Above all I call you to be intercessors.'

Two years later a prophecy was sent to us by one of our readers, Joan Gordon Farleigh, a vicar's wife from Harrogate Yorkshire. This word seemed to be fully in line with the words we had received at Carmel and Jerusalem foreshadowing a time of great shaking that would affect all nations. It was a warning note that we believed ought to be made public.

TIME OF TRIAL

January 1988

Thus says the Lord, 'I am about to shake the earth, to shake the nations, and to sift you as wheat is sifted. I will separate the chaff from the wheat.

'As I did in the land of Egypt so will I do with you. I will make a difference between those who are my people and those who belong to the gods of this world.

'Turn to me with all your heart and put away your idols from among you; deal righteously and justly in all that you do, for you are mine, and my name which is holy shall be honoured and uplifted among you.

'I am about to bring a time of great trial upon the world, but you who obey me will know my favour and my protection. There will be weeping and wailing and great distress all around you, but your needs will be supplied when all the systems of this world fail. All people will see that I care for you, but only as you obey me and sanctify me in your hearts.'

Another prophecy that has been widely accepted and reproduced is a word given by David Noakes in November 1994 warning of difficult times coming upon the faithful remnant of Bible believing Christians in the Western nations. It was far-seeing in that the forces of secular humanism were not very far advanced at that stage and there was no threat to the personal freedom of Christians to speak freely in the public square.

David was hearing warnings from God that the days were coming when Christians would not be allowed to speak about their faith in public, or to offer to pray for people in the workplace. At that time, any such predictions of difficult times for Christians, or of persecution of Christians in Western nations seemed to come from the world of fantasy, but we published this prophecy believing it to be a true word from God.

WALKING ON WATER

A prophecy to leaders in the church

November 1994

'In the days which are to come, that part of the church which will survive and prevail as overcomers will be that part which has learned to walk upon the waters, trusting only in me. There will be such storms that it will no longer be possible, as it were, to cross the waters by the ordinary means of using a boat, for the storms will be such that any boat will founder.

'The ways of traditional church organisation will not be adequate for the needs, because they will be too rigid and inflexible to withstand the wind and the waves, and those who have put their trust in them for their security will be like those who find themselves in a boat which is overwhelmed and doomed to sink.

'In those days only those who have learned to walk upon the waters will walk in safety. Do not put my people into rigid formal structures, for to do this is to put them into a boat which will seem adequate and comfortable while the waters are calm, but will later become a place of death for those whose only experience has been to get in and enjoy the ride.

'The structure of my church is not to be like a ship, a monolithic whole, a structure created by men. It is to be my body, a thing which is completely mobile and flexible, able to respond and adapt to the needs of the moment.

'A body will survive; but any structure created through the wisdom and efforts of man will prove to be like the ship which will sink in the time of trouble and pressure. Do not over-organise my people but teach them the ways of God; teach them the way of listening for the voice of my Spirit, and of spontaneous action in obedience to those promptings.

'Teach them not to rely upon men, or upon any form of organised structure, but teach them that each one must have his trust solely in me, the Head of the body, who alone has the wisdom to guide his people through the stormy waters.

'The days are coming when every item of your security which depends upon the ways of man and the structures of the world will be taken from you. No matter how hard you have laboured to build it up and no matter how much my people have asked me to bless it, it will all be like having placed your treasure in a bank which has suddenly closed its doors to you and will permit you no access.

'Teach my people, therefore, the way of walking on the water. Teach them in these days while the waters are yet calm to put their eyes upon me with a whole-hearted intensity.'

The next prophecy in this short selection of words published in the printed magazine *Prophecy Today* was given by the Revd Graham Blyth who was the Rector of St John the Baptist Anglican Church, Danbury, Essex. The background of this word was the increasing secularisation of Britain through the laws that were passed in our Parliament. Its relevance here is because that is the subject of our next chapter. This word was given at a time when family breakdown was accelerating, worship in state day schools and the teaching of biblical Christianity were all being neglected. A tide of lawlessness was spreading across the nation and this word was a clear call for repentance.

YOU HAVE FORGOTTEN ME

June 1998

'You have set the children's teeth on edge. You have taken from them the innocence I gave them when I entrusted them to you. You have deprived the children of their bread – their right to know my laws, to have them inscribed on their hearts.

'Your own hearts are far from me and you have forgotten me. In the West you have set up the idols of commerce and greed, and your children are practised in the arts of self-advancement. You depend on Mammon for your security: you ignore the poor and the destitute. In your confusion you turn to pagan beliefs and old superstitions in pursuit of happiness and success, but all these blessings will elude you. You work seven days in the week and you will experience the effects of your own madness in stress and disease.

'Many children whose families are breaking up will not forgive you in years to come. Their hearts will be hardened, their spirits full of revenge for the childhood that was ravished from them. They will turn against you and against one another: there will be no more loyalty, but only betrayal, with every man for himself. There will be loneliness and despair on a scale never seen before, and the heavens will be as brass.

'Only a remnant who are faithful to me will be saved. They will be ridiculed and mocked for their allegiance to me, but I will never forsake them. They will be oppressed and they will suffer on account of the rising tide of lawlessness.

'My word will judge the nations and those who reject and abuse me.

'The British people have cast me aside and it will confound them. Only repent, and my *love* will restore and rebuild you.'

A WORD FROM DAVID NOAKES

17th June 2017

My colleague David Noakes and I both heard similar words back in the 1980s that there would be a new move of God coming out of days of darkness. So, I want to end this chapter with a word that David gave at a meeting in East Grinstead that expresses these thoughts. But I want to re-emphasise that modern prophecy does not carry the authority of Scripture, although the Bible sets the standard of truth whereby any modern words purporting to have come from God must be tested. All genuine words have to go through human minds which inevitably affects the way the thoughts are expressed. Human beings who are in a close relationship with God through faithful devotion, intercession, and study of the Bible, may receive thoughts which they express in their own words which reflect something of what God is saying to us today.

This is the word that was given to David:

'Beloved, you are living in momentous days. These are truly the days of a turning point in the affairs of your nation. It is a time of my appointing. I have allowed you to go your own way, but I have never let go of you.

'There are many voices in your midst which are full of pessimism and I understand that if you look upon your circumstances, pessimism is often the outcome. But I want you to perceive as I perceive.

'Beloved, when there is turmoil and upheaval, do not look upon it with dismay; do not look upon it with foreboding; do not look upon it with fear. But look upon it with eyes turned to me with a questioning heart: a heart questioning what your God is doing in the midst of it. For beloved, all these things taking place are under my hand. I have brought about a remarkable work in your nation in recent times. This is not accidental nor is it sudden, but it has come about at my appointed time.

'I do not have accidents; I do not have coincidences; I do not have sudden unexpected events. I have appointed events, at appointed times, and I am the one who is seated in the heavens and does whatever he pleases. Do not lose heart, because I am in charge. My hand is on your nation and I have not given up my purposes for you.

'I have blessed your nation in the past and truly you have been faithless; but beloved, I have remained faithful. Your enemy has done much to sow lies, to sow false doctrine, to try to bring down all that is good and all that is of God. But I have kept for myself a remnant. My word remains true for all time and all eternity and I will fulfil my purposes.

'This is a time of turmoil and upheaval because your adversary is in great rage and great fear. He is in great consternation that I will use your nation to tear his purposes apart. But that is exactly what I intend to do. I intend to bring his purposes crashing down. There will be turmoil and upheaval; there will be blood in the streets; there will be anxiety amongst those who do not know that God is in charge and do not understand what I am doing.

'Beloved there cannot be victory in war without war taking place; and war is indeed taking place, because I have joined battle. I have joined battle against the forces of darkness which desire to bring your nation to nothing, and I have declared I will not have it so. My purposes for you are from eternity. I have known exactly what I will do at this time. I have known exactly what I will do in the future and I purpose to glorify my name through your nation once again.

'Therefore, do not be disheartened. Do you think of yourself as being just a little flock? Truly there is only a small remnant who hold fast to my word. But beloved, continue to hold fast to my word and pray that the purposes that I have begun to reveal will come to fruition and fulfilment, and I will visit you afresh with my Spirit.

'I will visit you afresh with my Spirit so that you may be empowered: not for your glory, but for mine. Not to build empires, but to build my church. I desire also to visit you with my Spirit that you may be instruments in my hand to go into the fields which are ripe for harvest, and bring in a harvest; for there is a harvest waiting to be brought in.

'There are many in fear and trepidation and utter confusion, and I want you to be a people who know their God and do exploits. I want you to be a people of compassion, not of judgment, not of condemnation. Judgement is mine, I will repay. But I ask you to be a people of love and concern; of compassion for the lost, and of deep desire that the truth should be brought to many who will understand it and be saved. For surely there are those among you whom you think are your enemies; but who are longing for truth.

'Do not be downhearted, therefore, do not be dispirited. Yes, I know all too well that you are surrounded by those who wish you ill. Beloved, do not heed them, but look to your God who wishes you well. Look to your God who wishes them well. I desire a people who are willing to bless their enemies and to do good to those who speak evil about them.'

CHAPTER 7

THE SECULARISATION OF BRITAIN

Witchcraft

The slow process of the secularisation of Britain began in the 1950s with Acts of Parliament at the beginning and end of the decade that would have a profound effect upon the life of the nation in decades to come. The first Act was the **1951 Fraudulent Mediums Act** which abolished the ancient **Witchcraft Act** that had banned all forms of witchcraft in Britain for hundreds of years.

At that time this was seen as a harmless piece of social legislation getting rid of an outdated law that had no relevance today. But it opened the way for a wide range of occult activities from witches' covens to Ouija boards. Its effect was not just to ban fraudulent witchcraft activities, but to legalise genuine witchcraft! Throughout the Bible witchcraft is condemned in all its different forms. Moses set the template for this in his list of detestable practices that the people were to avoid when they reached the promised land. He said:

"When you enter the land the Lord your God is giving you, do not learn to imitate the detestable ways of the nations there. Let no one be found among you who sacrifices his son or daughter in the fire, who practises divination or sorcery, interprets omens, engages in witchcraft, or casts spells, or is a medium, or spiritualist, or who consults the dead. Anyone who does these things is detestable to the Lord, and because of these detestable practices the Lord your God will drive out those nations before you" (Deut 18:9-12).

The prophets of Israel were strong in their condemnation of all forms of idolatry. Jeremiah, in his famous 'Temple Sermon', berated the people of Jerusalem who were baking cakes of bread for the Queen of Heaven and pouring out drink offerings to foreign gods. They had even set up detestable idols in the temple and built shrines in the *"Valley of Ben Hinnom to burn their sons and daughters in the fire"* (Jer 7:31).

In the New Testament there are many references to idolatry and warnings to Christians to avoid any form of worshipping idols or even of eating food that had been sacrificed to idols. Paul lists idolaters among those who will not inherit the kingdom of God (1 Cor 6:9), and he sees idolatry as the first step in the corruption of human civilization (Rom 1:24-32).

Obscenity

The second Act in the 1950s was **The Obscene Publications Act 1959**. It was full of ambiguity and caused confusion among parliamentarians for decades to come. The problem lay in its definition of obscenity as "a tendency to corrupt and deprave". During the video nasties campaign when I was the leader of the 'research group' for the Parliamentary Inquiry Team I discovered numerous occasions where county courts were unable to deliver a clear judgment on infringements of the law because a defence lawyer appealed to the jury who had just been shown excerpts from films depicting explicit sex or violence.

They were then asked if this had corrupted them. Of course, no one wished to admit that they had been corrupted, so the prosecution were unable to obtain convictions, particularly if they had a number of young men on the jury. Numerous times MPs tried to amend the law but could not find an acceptable definition of obscenity. The law came before the House of Commons for amendment in 1964, again in 1977, and as part of the Broadcasting Act 1990, with numerous attempts at Private Members' Bills, or Bills in the House of Lords, all of which failed. The finest minds in the British Parliament were unable to find a satisfactory definition of 'obscenity'!

In **1968 The Theatres Act** virtually abolished censorship in the theatre, although public performances of plays still required licensing and 'obscene' performances were prohibited. Nevertheless, with Parliament being unable to define 'obscenity' this left a gaping hole in the legal requirements for acceptable standards of what could be presented to the public. It actually allowed nudity and explicit sexual acts on stage and thus paved the way for the vast ocean of pornography that was to flood the Internet.

Abortion

There were three other Acts of Parliament in the 1960s each of which were of ground-breaking significance in advancing the secularisation of the nation. The first was **The Abortion Act 1967.** The death penalty for murder had been abolished in 1965 but this Act said that it was socially acceptable to kill unborn babies. The Bill was introduced into the House of Commons by Liberal MP David Steel as a Private Member's Bill which enabled it to slip through the House of Commons on Fridays when few MPs were present and there was very little public debate.

The Act allowed babies to be aborted up to 28 weeks' gestation. This was later changed, allowing abortions up to 20 weeks, but also allowing for the abortion of disabled babies at a much later stage in the pregnancy. Northern Ireland was exempted from the Abortion Act until January 2020 when it became law under a procedural default of the Northern Ireland Assembly to reconvene Stormont in time to stop it.

The Abortion Act has resulted in the death of some nine million babies since 1967 and shows society's disregard for the sanctity of human life. It runs contrary to the repeated condemnation in the Bible of the shedding of innocent blood which was constantly referred to by the Biblical prophets. The widespread practice in Britain of abortions for no medical reasons has allowed it to be used as a socially acceptable form of contraception whereby aborted babies are put into a black bag and taken out of the back of hospitals and clinics to be cast into an incinerator at the end of each working day.

The practice of burning babies in the fire is roundly condemned in the Bible as being detestable to God. Jeremiah expressed shock and horror at the practice in the valley outside Jerusalem that he called the 'Valley of Slaughter' (Jer 7:32). Throughout the history of Israel, the shedding of innocent blood was condemned. It was one of the warnings given by Moses, *"You must purge from Israel the guilt of shedding innocent blood, so that it may go well with you"* (Deut 19:13).

Sexual Offences

The same year as the Abortion Act was passed, also saw the passing of another ground-breaking law, the **Sexual Offences Act 1967**, which legalised homosexual activity between consenting males over the age of 21. The age of consent was reduced to 18 as part of **The Criminal Justice and Public Order Act 1994.** Then six years later **The Sexual Offences Amendment Act 2000,** equalised the age of consent for homosexual and heterosexual practices at 16. All this was in direct contradiction of Biblical teaching on sexual relationships going back to the time of Moses where a range of prohibitions were added to the Law for the protection of the health and wellbeing of society. The law in Leviticus 18:22 was quite uncompromising, *"Do not lie with a man as one lies with a woman; that is detestable".*

Biblical prohibition of homosexual acts was both a health and a creation issue. In terms of health it was for the protection of individual men, as the human body is not created for anal intercourse which results in bleeding and a range of infections. It is also a creation issue in that sexual intercourse is given for the procreation of human life and if there were widespread homosexual practices the human race would die out. Homosexuality is a form of social suicide.

In New Testament times the teaching on sexual relationships was equally firm and uncompromising. Paul routinely mixes homosexual acts with other sinful activities. He said,

"Neither the sexually immoral nor idolaters nor adulterers nor male prostitutes nor homosexual offenders nor thieves nor the greedy nor drunkards nor slanderers will inherit the kingdom of God" (1 Cor 6:9-10).

Undermining the Family

Both the **Abortion Act** and the **Sexual Offences Act** had an indirect effect upon the health and stability of **the family** which is the most important of all five major social institutions in supporting and upholding the structures of society.[9] The final blow of the decade

---

9 The five major social institutions supporting the structure and function of society, recognised by sociologists are: The Family, The Economy, Law and Government, Education and Religion. Any change occurring in any one of these affects all the others. Of these five, most sociologists would agree that the family is the most significant in terms of the health, wellbeing and stability of society.

was a direct attack upon the family in **The Divorce Reform Act 1969.** This Act introduced the principle of the irretrievable breakdown of marriage as the sole ground for divorce.

As proof of marriage breakdown, a range of issues were acceptable, such as adultery, unreasonable behaviour of either spouse, or desertion; or by separation of at least two years provided there was the consent of both parties. Without such a consent a separation of five years was required for a divorce. Inevitably, this Act opened the way for easier divorce and the immediate social effect was a significant rise in the divorce rate.

From that time family breakdown became socially acceptable with a devastating effect upon the lives of millions of children who were the innocent victims of their parents' unfaithfulness. The disintegration of the family was the objective of the homosexual lobby. **In 1971 they issued a Manifesto** declaring that their ultimate objective was **the destruction of the traditional family.** I was a Senior Lecturer in Sociology in London University in 1971 when I was handed a copy of the leaflet. I laughed when I read that statement, thinking that it was unachievable, but their progress since then has been unbelievable.[10]

Sunday schools and Churches

The secularisation of Britain entered a new phase that was accelerated by the decline in church attendance and the even more rapid decline of Sunday school attendance. In the 1950s some three quarters of the nation's children went to Sunday school, but by the end of the 1960s there was a total collapse of afternoon Sunday schools.

Most churches changed to the provision for children's worship in their regular Sunday morning services, but this only reached the children of regular churchgoers and the churches lost contact with vast numbers of families whose main contact with the church had been through their children's attendance at afternoon Sunday school. The mission of the church became inward – only reaching those who were already committed Christians. At the same time major cultural changes were taking place in the nation. We changed our recreational

---

10 See the last chapter of this book for further information on the Gay Liberation Front Manifesto.

habits to Sunday day trips to the seaside and beauty spots. Sunday worship as a sacred Sabbath was abandoned. The influence of our Judeo-Christian faith began a steep decline.

Day Schools

The Education Act 1996 required all children attending a maintained school, other than a special school, to take part in a collective act of Christian worship each day but it was found to be increasingly difficult to find teachers able to comply with this requirement. By the end of the century these requirements were all effectively repealed and even the basic elements of biblical Christianity were no longer taught to children in our national day schools.

During the 30 year period from 1960 to 1990 there was still a strong element of Christian faith and teaching in the nation. The Judeo-Christian heritage was strong in the middle and older generations who held power and influence in the nation, but their influence was never mobilised effectively in defence of Biblical morality, despite the valiant efforts of morality groups such as the Festival of Light led by Malcolm Muggeridge and Mary Whitehouse.

Morality Groups

These groups never enjoyed the official backing of church leaders and in hindsight it is probably true to say that the single most significant element in the secularisation of Britain during this period was the failure of church leaders to defend the family as an essential element in God's creation. I have written elsewhere about this in *The Reshaping of Britain* but it is worth quoting here because of its significance.

"The nadir of the lifelong monogamous family was reached in July 2000. The Government's Green paper *Supporting Families* had correctly stated that marriage was the most reliable framework for raising children. A peer attempted to include that statement in the Education Bill going through Parliament so that all children would be taught that the married family is the ideal.

Writing about this political incident, sociologist Norman Dennis said, "The ecclesiastical historian of the future might well take the view that 18 July 2000, was a landmark in the development of the Church of England's attitude to holy matrimony. Nine bishops voted against the amendment. If they had voted the other way the amendment would have been carried."[11]

It is incredible that although there were nine bishops in the House of Lords on that July day in 2000, they all voted against putting into law that children should be taught that a married couple family is the ideal family unit. This is a truth with overwhelming research-based factual evidence to support it (as well as the Bible!) and the Bishops should not have been afraid of displeasing the LGBT+ lobby by declaring the truth! It was either an act of gross cowardice that richly deserved the judgment of God upon the state church, or it was a deliberate betrayal of their responsibilities as representatives of the church and spokesmen for God.

Europe

The most far-reaching legislation of the 1970s was **The European Communities Act 1972** which was followed by its Amendment Acts of 1986 and 1993. This Act took Britain into the European Economic Community (EEC) as it was at that time, and the subsequent amendments took us deeper into the European Union. This meant losing our national sovereignty; and losing control of our borders and the fishing rights of our fishermen in our own coastal waters. It also meant conforming to European agricultural laws and a vast array of regulations issued by Brussels.

This was probably the most controversial law passed by a British parliament in the 20th century. It also increased the strength of secularisation in Britain as the European Union refused to have any mention of Christianity in its constitution. It caused enormous division in the nation that has never been healed. The division rumbled on until David Cameron felt obliged to give the nation an IN/OUT referendum and the unexpected narrow majority to leave the EU produced the ongoing controversy surrounding Brexit.

---

11 Clifford Hill, *The Reshaping of Britain: Church and State since the 1960s, A Personal Reflection*, Wilberforce Publications, London, 2018, page 311.

Children

The Children Act 1989 was the next Act of Parliament to give a further twist in the spiral of secularisation. The intention of the Act was to give greater protection to children, particularly to those who were vulnerable to abuse. Its effect, however was to remove the traditional concept of parental responsibility for children and handed considerable power to the state, providing for children to be removed from parents if social workers deemed them to be unfit, or if the children were in danger of child abuse.

In handing power to the state for the teaching of children the nation was moving farther away from the whole concept of parental responsibility that is embedded in our Judeo-Christian heritage which is neatly summed up in the *shema*:

"Hear, O Israel: The Lord our God, the Lord is one. Love the Lord your God with all your heart and with all your soul and with all your strength. These commandments that I give you today are to be upon your hearts. Impress them on your children. Talk about them when you sit at home and when you walk along the road, when you lie down and when you get up" (Deut 6:4-7).

This Biblical admonition to teach the faith to our children was developed strongly during the exile in Babylon in the fifth century BC. After the destruction of the temple in Jerusalem, the people of Judah in exile could no longer rely upon the formal prayers of the priests. They had to discover a new relationship with God which they found in prayer in their homes, where both boys and girls were educated until the age of ten, after which the boys went to the local village meeting hall or Knesset.[12]

It was in their homes that the children were taught the history of Israel and the giving of the law to Moses. This was where they learned portions of the Torah, sang psalms, and on Friday evenings they enjoyed a Sabbath meal around the family table. It was here, in the family homes of the people in exile, that the faith of the people of Israel was preserved.

---

12 The Knesset, local community meeting place during the Babylonian exile, later became known as the Synagogue during the Greek period.

In New Testament times there was a similarity with the exile. It was in the home-based fellowships that the believers in Jesus as Messiah began among Messianic Jews and then spread to the Gentiles. The solidarity of the family played an important role in the spread of Christianity and parents took their responsibilities of teaching their children so seriously that during times of persecution when many believers were martyred, they appointed godparents to ensure that their children were taught their faith and the gospel was preserved to the next generation.

In Britain, the older generation of senior citizens whose children were born since 1960 and who have lived through the time of rapid social change and intensive secularisation either did not regard it as the duty of parents to teach the faith to their children, or if they did, they were highly unsuccessful. Even committed Christian parents did not take seriously the responsibility to teach the faith to their children in their homes as in Jewish households. Christians simply expected their children to grow into the faith because Britain was a Christian country or left it to others. Hence the great falling away in what is now the middle-age generation.

Church leaders did not stress the importance of parents sharing their faith with their children and the general assumption was that the children would learn all that was necessary at school. So, it was not only the law that transferred responsibility for children from parents to the state; but both church and Christian parents tacitly agreed with such a policy, and when the schools were no longer able, or willing, to teach the Christian faith to children – nobody taught them! So we have a generation of young people who are biblically illiterate and have never heard the gospel, in a country, which in the Victorian era, was the leading missionary nation in the world.

Life Issues

The 1990s saw a number of Acts of Parliament that were directly contrary to the teaching of the Bible, and they increased the secularisation of the nation, turning away from a commitment to upholding Biblical truth.

The Human Fertilisation and Embryology Act 1999 was passed by Parliament, allowing experimentation on human embryos as well as their storage for future use by individuals. This Act also amended **The Abortion Act 1967**, resulting in abortion on demand for handicapped babies right up to the time of birth. It was a major step forward in the secularisation of the nation and a deliberate act of defiance of the God of Creation who declared that he had created human beings in his own image. As a nation we said that we no longer respected the sanctity of human life and we gave our scientists freedom to experiment with the aborted babies we would otherwise have thrown into the incinerator.

Sunday Observance

The Sunday Trading Act 1993 was a severe blow to evangelical Christians who had strongly fought under the banner of "Keep Sunday Special". That campaign had been supported not only by Bible-believing Christians, but by shop workers and many other people who would be forced to work on Sundays rather than enjoying a day of rest or spending time with their families. It was the only Bill that Margaret Thatcher's Government lost in their first attempt, but they succeeded at their second attempt with the support of Opposition Parties, despite huge opposition from their own back benches.

Sundays became just like any other day with sporting events, places of entertainment and shops open. The whole concept of the Sabbath as a day of rest from work, a time for reflection and worship, was lost, disappearing into the realms of history as the nation swept on in an endless drive away from its Biblical roots. The Sabbath that was one of the Ten Commandments simply disappeared off the national radar.

As the Fourth Commandment, it was given the longest treatment setting out the requirements:

"Remember the Sabbath day by keeping it holy. Six days you shall labour and do all your work, but the seventh day is a Sabbath to the Lord your God. On it you shall not do any work, neither you, nor your son or daughter, nor your man servant or maidservant, nor your animals, nor the alien within your gates. For in six days the Lord made

the heavens and the earth, the sea and all that is in them. But he rested on the seventh day. Therefore, the Lord blessed the Sabbath day and made it holy" (Ex 20:8-11).

Being 'holy' of course, meant being *different* from all the other days in the week, but this was of no concern to the secular mind.

In the Torah it is stated that the Sabbath is a day of rest that must be obeyed because it is a *"lasting ordinance"* (Lev 16:31). Jeremiah said that the neglect of the Sabbath was one of the reasons why God was bringing judgment upon Jerusalem. He said that the word of the Lord was: *"Do not bring a load out of your houses or do any work on the Sabbath, but keep the Sabbath day holy, as I commanded your forefathers. Yet they did not listen or pay attention; they were stiff-necked and would not listen or respond to discipline"* (Jer 17:22-23).

Ezekiel also listed the desecration of the Sabbath among the reasons that led to God's decision to withdraw his covering of protection over Jerusalem: *"Her priests do violence to my law and profane my holy things; they do not distinguish between the holy and the common; they teach that there is no difference between the unclean and the clean; and they shut their eyes to the keeping of my Sabbaths, so that I am profaned among them"* (Ezek 22:26).

The decision to desecrate Sundays in defiance of the biblical command to keep the Sabbath day as a holy day to the Lord was amongst the most serious acts of defiance of the word of God in the 20th century.

Gambling

The following year **The National Lottery Act 1994** was passed to satisfy the nation's desire for big stakes gambling. As a sop to those who opposed gambling, a portion of the proceeds was allocated for 'good causes' which included the preservation of ancient buildings as part of the nation's cultural heritage, but the spiritual heritage of the nation was further neglected. This encouraged many more people to become addicted to gambling with a devastating effect upon a minority of persistent gamblers.

In Paul's letter to Timothy he warns about the dangers of seeking to become rich. He says, *"People who want to get rich fall into temptation and a trap and into many foolish and harmful desires that plunge men into ruin and destruction. For the love of money is a root of all kinds of evil. Some people, eager for money, have wandered from the faith and pierced themselves with many griefs"* (1 Tim 6:9-10).

Levels of personal debt increased in the nation with the use of credit cards soaring. It had the additional effect of increasing the overall level of national debt, with large numbers of people living with a lifestyle beyond their means. Far from helping the poor, the Lottery increased the national level of poverty.

Finance

The Finance Act 1999 was one of those Acts of Parliament that slipped through the Commons without very much public attention, but it dealt a significant blow to both family and marriage. It removed the married person's allowance, thereby further degrading the value of marriage. This was at a time when divorce rates were at the highest on record, and family breakdown was causing a wide range of social problems. It was a time when the Lords and Commons Family and Child Protection Group (of which I was the Convenor and Research Director) produced a series of reports on the health of the family, all drawing attention to the need for strengthening the marriage-based family as the healthiest and most stable form of family life.

In July 1998 we published the report *Family Matters* with detailed research warning of the consequences of ignoring the trends. Home Secretary Jack Straw promised a White Paper and legislation strengthening marriage and family life but the pressures within the Cabinet and from the backbenches prevented this. The Government led by Tony Blair had a number of women who had experienced unhappy marriages and gave strong support to measures calling for 'equality' in all forms of family regardless of the statistical evidence in favour of marriage. It was at this time that the LGBT lobby began to gain significant influence among civil servants in Whitehall as well as among MPs. The processes of secularisation gained a significant momentum.

Equality and the Family

The Civil Partnership Act 2004 was a huge milestone in the advancement of secularisation and the weakening of the family in Britain. It was the beginning of the 'equality movement' that swept all before it in the early years of the 21st century. The Act gave Civil Partnerships the same rights and responsibilities as that of civil heterosexual marriage. It was another step in undermining the value of the marriage-based family.

It was quickly followed in the same year by **The Gender Recognition Act 2004** that granted transsexual people the same legal recognition as members of the opposite sex to their birth gender either male or female. This was another massive step in undermining marriage and traditional family life. It was a direct attack upon God's act of creation in which he said that he created men and women in his own image. The Genesis account of creation says:

"Then God said, let us make man in our image, in our likeness, and let them rule over the fish of the sea and the birds in the air, over the livestock, over all the earth, and over all creatures that move along the ground" (Gen 1:26).

It was God's intention to create human beings different from all the rest of his creation with the ability to have communication and an intimate relationship with him. This Act, inspired by secular humanists, had the deliberate intention of undermining the Biblical account of creation in support of an evolutionist view of the universe.

This is part of the age of rebellion of humanity against God that is reflected in Palm 2 that says *"Why do the nations conspire and the people's plot in vain?. . ."* But *"The One enthroned in heaven laughs; the Lord scoffs at them"* (Ps 2:1-4). Isaiah says, *"The wisdom of the wise will perish, the intelligence of the intelligent will vanish. Woe to those who go to great depths to hide their plans from the Lord . . . You turn things upside down, as if the potter were thought to be like the clay! Shall what is formed say to him who formed it, 'He did not make me'?"* (Is 29:15-16).

The Apostle Paul says something similar in his letter to the Christians in Corinth who were proud of their great learning and wisdom. He said: *"For the foolishness of God is wiser than man's wisdom, and the weakness of God is stronger than man's strength"* (1 Cor 1:25). Paul's words are very apposite since the objective of the socio-political drive for 'equality' is to oppose the whole concept of the God of Creation.

Equality

The Equality Movement came to a head with **The Equality Acts 2006 and 2010. The 2006 Act created The Equality and Human Rights Commission (EHRC).** And **the 2010 Act** drew together all the other acts that had relevance to equality and human rights, bringing British law into line with **European Equal Treatment Directives.** This was a major objective of the secular humanists in the British Parliament because this brought Britain under the control of the European Union with its strong stand against Christianity and the teaching of the Bible.

Their particular hatred was directed against the God of the Bible who created the gender differences between male and female that were a major blockage to the objectives of the Gay Liberation lobby. If they were to achieve their objectives, biblical Christianity had to be discredited, and by aligning British law with the directives of the European Union on the subject of equality, they knew that this would be a major step forward towards achieving their goals.

This is undoubtedly one of the major reasons why Brexit was so strongly opposed by secular humanists and atheists. They had to keep Britain in line with the EU at all costs. Hence the passionate anger of the demonstrations inside and outside Parliament and on the streets of our cities. But the roots of Brexit go back much farther. In 2010 at the Conservative Conference David Cameron announced his intention of introducing same-sex marriage on the grounds of equality. This, of course, was a huge deception because there can be no equality between the faithful love union of a male and female couple who dedicate their lives to each other and to the procreation and raising of children, with the homosexual relationship of two men or two women.

David Cameron knew that it was the intention of the leaders of the European Union to make the legalisation of homosexual relationships legal in all EU nations, and he was determined to be ahead of the political game. His Coalition arrangement with the Liberal Democrats suited him very well as it enabled him to achieve his objective despite the opposition of more than 100 of his own backbenchers. The combined vote of the Lib Dems and Labour drove the Bill through Parliament in 2013.

Same Sex Marriage

The bitter division created by **The Marriage (Same Sex Couples) Act 2013** was behind much of the vitriolic debates in Parliament on Brexit issues that resulted from the 'In/Out' Referendum on the European Union of 2016. Subsequent events in the House of Commons confirmed this. The Parliament that Theresa May inherited was the most rebellious faced by a British Prime Minister for centuries. The angry scenes in debates broadcast to the world by television were a disgrace for the Mother of Parliaments and made Britain a laughingstock of the world.

The secular humanists led the way in these debates with atheists like Sir Kier Starmer (who is reported to have said that he regrets his parents naming him after Kier Hardie, the Christian founder of the Labour Party) leading opposition in the Brexit debate on a deal with the EU negotiated by Theresa May.

Of course, the Brexit issue did not end with the December 2019 election of Boris Johnson with a majority that confounded all the pundits. His success was undoubtedly a major victory for those who wished to separate Britain from the European Union with its strongly secularist agenda. But the battle is not yet concluded. There is a mountain of legislation that is offensive to God, that has been put onto the statute book of Britain in the past 40 years.

If the calls for repentance generated by the coronavirus pandemic were to bear any fruit this would have to be tackled by our politicians. Undoing the mountain of offensive legislation would be an incredible burden for any Prime Minister to face, even if there was plenty of public goodwill, particularly one who has not publicly acknowledged God in his own life and whose lifestyle is anything but that of a professing Christian.

In the next chapter we will look at the situation facing Britain in the middle of the Coronavirus Pandemic.

CHAPTER 8

THE WORLD IN REBELLION

Black Lives Matter

The death of George Floyd in police custody in Minneapolis in the USA in May 2020 triggered an eruption of protests not just across America but across the world. It produced the slogan 'Black Lives Matter' that was reproduced in countless demonstrations worldwide, even in cities where few black people were resident.

How did such a mass protest movement develop so rapidly and so widely, with millions of people taking to the streets? Many people felt passionate anger at the brutality of the police action in arresting a black man for a non-violent offence and deliberately killing him by kneeling on his neck for 9 minutes. The video of this heinous offence spread rapidly around the world triggering the demonstrations.

In America, the police headquarters in Minneapolis was burned to the ground and in many other cities severe rioting took place with arson and vandalised buildings, cars and other property. There were calls for the police to be defunded in a number of American states as public anger spread. The rioting went on for a number of days and was widely criticised by many commentators; but it also stimulated a national debate on the treatment of black people and those of mixed race whose heritage could be traced back to the days of slavery.

This debate was long overdue in America as little progress had been made since the assassination of Martin Luther King in 1968 in dealing with the systemic racism in police dealings with black people, since the days when they captured runaway slaves and returned them to their masters. Police attitudes are a reflection of the general culture in America whereby the black population lag behind the white population in most spheres of life such as health, employment, education and social status.

Race Relations

In Britain considerable progress has been made since the 1960s in changing attitudes towards black people from the early days of immigration where it was common to see adverts for accommodation with the words, 'NO COLOURED'. I have been involved in race relations for the whole of my working life. My first book in 1958, was called "BLACK AND WHITE IN HARMONY" with the subtitle *"The Drama of West Indians in the Big City from a London Minister's Notebook"*.[13] It was published in the same month as the Notting Hill riots in London which pitchforked my church into the public eye and resulted in me doing numerous radio and TV programmes.

Legislation

So, although a great deal of progress has been made through legislation to control discrimination in the workplace and in public, it is much more difficult to change attitudes and to eliminate racism from all sectors of society. Black leaders in Britain say that there are just sufficient black people in prominent positions in society to convince the white population that all is well.

Statistics support their experience by showing that children of West Indian descent perform badly in educational achievement in comparison with white children. There are many reasons for this but the research in which I have been involved shows clearly that much of this underachievement and health issues can be traced back to slavery as part of the heritage of Caribbean people who suffered 300 years of slavery in British Colonies.

Colonialism

Historically Britain was one of the earliest European nations to participate in the slave trade. Edward Colston was a director, and became Deputy Governor of the Royal African Company, the largest of the seventeenth century European slave traders. Hence the outpourings of anger on the streets of Bristol as he is reported to have been responsible for transporting 80,000 Africans across the Atlantic

---

13 Clifford Hill, *'Black and White in Harmony'*, Hodder and Stoughton, London 1958.

to spend a lifetime in enforced slavery enduring the monumental cruelty of the plantations which usually resulted in death at a young age. Many people in America blamed Britain for exporting their attitudes of white superiority to the USA and to many other nations around the world.

Many Caribbean people did not like the film 'Amazing Grace' about the abolition campaign led by William Wilberforce in the late 18th century that resulted in the abolition of the slave trade in 1807. They saw the focus too much upon the work of the white abolitionists in London whereas the African activists on the slave plantations in the Caribbean were not featured in the film which they saw as further evidence of white superiority.

From the time of the Mansfield Declaration in 1772 establishing in law that anyone who set foot in Britain was a free person, there had been a sense of moral superiority, which was increased when Britain became the first nation in Europe to abandon slavery in its Colonies. This reinforced British pride in its national righteousness, which reinforced attitudes of white supremacy and paternalism towards black people.

History of Slavery

For 200 years the history of colonial slavery was not taught in British schools. If there was any mention of slavery it was about the cotton fields in America and not about the sugar plantations in British colonies in Jamaica, Barbados and other Caribbean islands. Most white British people are quite unaware of the innate nationalism and pride that is part of our human nature and they cannot enter into the experience of young black people in Britain today who grow up in a world where they are made to feel inferior and treated as second-class citizens. Many black people deeply resent the indignity of being stopped by the police simply because they lack the protection of being white.

It should not be surprising that resentment spilled out onto the streets of many cities throughout Britain. Memorials such as the statue of Colston in Bristol were a constant reminder of white supremacy and the fact that the City of Bristol was built upon the proceeds of the slave trade. But so too were London and Liverpool and many other cities. In the year 1800, seven years before the abolition of the slave trade, two thirds of the national economy of Britain was said to be connected with colonial slavery in some way, which is no doubt the reason why it was so difficult for the abolitionists to persuade Parliament to stop the slave trade which was considered to be the economic lifeline of the nation.

It is quite understandable that for some members of the black community the opportunity to throw the bronze figure of Colston into the Harbour from which his ships sailed was a cathartic moment. But removing the statute does not erase the history of British slavery. Neither does it deal with attitudes of white superiority and innate pride.

The Influence of Anarchy

The demonstrations calling for justice for black people although understandable as an expression of outrage against police brutality were much more complex. Many groups of anarchists and others with an anti-social agenda took the opportunity of joining in the protests. The spirit of rebellion that was publicly released onto the streets was not new to the 21st century. In Britain it goes back at least to the time of the Enlightenment and has a deeply spiritual, as well as a social content.

The weeks of lockdown generated by the coronavirus pandemic, undoubtedly stirred deep resentments and frustration, exacerbated for many people by losing their jobs, or being faced with an uncertain future. But the spiritual element in the anarchy that was seen in the violent behaviour of some people in the demonstrations, is deeply rooted in a spirit of rebellion in human nature. It is not only rebellion against the rule of law, but it is rebellion against the God of Creation that is deeply embedded in our human nature and goes back to the Fall of mankind.

Psalm 55 expresses concern that this spirit of rebellion can spill over onto the city streets. It says:

"I see violence and strife in the city. Day and night they prowl about on its walls; malice and abuse are within it. Destructive forces are at work in the city; threats and lies never leave its streets" (Ps 55:9-11).

It is these destructive forces that the Psalmist sees at work in the city which form the spirit of anarchy and rebellion – not just against the forces of law and order in the city, but against the God of Creation. This spirit lies behind the theme of Psalm 2 which says:

"Why do the nations conspire and the peoples plot in vain? The kings of the earth take their stand and the rulers gather together against the Lord and against his Anointed One. Let us break their chains, they say, and throw off their fetters."

The Man of Lawlessness

The Psalmist sees God scoffing at them for the futility of their rebellious spirit which cannot succeed against the sovereignty of God who will work out his purposes despite all the opposition from human sources. In the New Testament we are told that God actually holds backs the forces of destruction that are at work in society until the time of his choosing.

Paul describes this spirit of rebellion as being under the control of God who will hold it back until the days leading up to the second coming of Jesus.

"Don't let anyone deceive you in any way," he says. *"For that day will not come until the rebellion occurs and the man of lawlessness is revealed, the man doomed to destruction."* Paul also says, *"For the secret power of lawlessness is already at work; but the one who now holds it back will continue to do so till he is taken out of the way"* (2 Thes 2:3-7).

In the same chapter Paul also says, *"The coming of the lawless one will be in accordance with the work of Satan displayed in all kinds of counterfeit miracles, signs and wonders, and in every sort of evil that deceives those who are perishing"* (2 Thes 2:9).

A Powerful Delusion

We are certainly seeing plenty of deception with fake news spread rapidly by social media that is believed by millions. The power of the media to influence public opinion and rouse anger sufficiently to take millions of people onto the streets has been demonstrated by the willingness of people to obey calls for direct action even despite the dangers of the coronavirus pandemic spreading. People are easily deceived, and every kind of evil follows when crowd behaviour removes individual caution. Paul talks about *"a powerful delusion"* being sent by God which becomes a part of the great shaking of the nations (2 Thes 2:11).

There are many other signs today indicating that we are nearing the kind of conditions described in the Bible as leading up to the days before the Second Coming of Christ. Jesus spoke of nation rising against nation, famines and earthquakes; and the persecution of believers, plus false prophets – all of which we are seeing in abundance today, and many more signs.

It certainly seems that what we are seeing in our lifetime is an increase in the spirit of rebellion in humanity on a worldwide scale. But rebellion is nothing new: all the prophets of Israel had to deal with rebellion, starting with Moses who had to lead the people through the desert for 40 years because they did not have the faith to trust God to take them into the land of Canaan when the little group of explorers came back and reported *"All the people we saw there are of great size"* (Num 13:32). Moses warned the people not to rebel against the Lord. *"Do not be afraid of the people in the land, because we will swallow them up. Their protection is gone, but the Lord is with us"* (Num 14:9). His warnings went unheeded and the consequence of their rebellion was a delay of 40 years in entering the promised land, and all the rebels died in the desert – only Joshua and Caleb were spared to enter Canaan.

Penalties for Rebellion

Jeremiah knew the penalties of rebellion against God. He describes in chapter 5 how he went up and down the streets of Jerusalem looking for people who dealt honestly and sought the truth, but he found that even the leaders had broken off their yoke with God; and they were a people in rebellion against the Lord.

Like Jeremiah, Ezekiel also told the people of Jerusalem that because of their rebellion against God, he would allow the Babylonians to conquer Jerusalem and take them into exile. He brought an uncompromising word from God:

"The end is now upon you and I will unleash my anger against you. I will judge you according to your conduct and repay you for all your detestable practices. I will not look on you with pity or spare you; I will surely repay you for your conduct and the detestable practices among you. Then you will know that I am the Lord" (Ezek 7:3-4).

In fact, Ezekiel, in a remarkable vision, actually went farther than saying that God would remove his cover of protection; he said that God would actually guide the Babylonian army to Jerusalem. He foresaw the Babylonians marching towards the West where at some point they would stop at a fork of the road, at the junction of two roads where he would seek an omen from his diviners as to which road he should take.

One road would take him south on the east side of the River Jordan to attack the Ammonites and the other road would take him down the West Bank to Jericho and then up to Jerusalem. Ezekiel said that God will guide Nebuchadnezzar to take the road to Jerusalem. *"Into his right hand will come the lot for Jerusalem, where he is to set up battering rams, to give the command to slaughter, to sound the battle cry, to set battering rams against the gates, to build a ramp and to erect siege works"* (Ezek 21:22).

Sins of Jerusalem

In the following chapter Ezekiel summarises the sins of the city of Jerusalem and her King. The sins range from oppressing the aliens, orphans and widows to desecrating the Sabbaths, practising idolatry, detestable sexual offences, shedding blood, and bribery and corruption. The list ends with the words, *"And you have forgotten me, declares the Sovereign Lord. I will surely strike my hands together at the unjust gain you have made and at the blood you have shed in your midst"* (Ezek 22:12-13).

Ezekiel even goes so far as to compare the sins of Judah with those of Sodom. He says *"You not only walked in their ways and copied their detestable practices, but in all your ways you soon became more depraved than they. As surely as I live, declares the Sovereign Lord, your sister Sodom and her daughters never did what you and your daughters have done"* (Ezek 16:47-48).

In a surprising statement he then says,

"Now this was the sin of your sister Sodom: she and her daughters were arrogant, overfed and unconcerned; they did not help the poor and needy. They were haughty and did detestable things before me. Therefore, I did away with them as you have seen."

Clearly the sins of Sodom were not only detestable sexual practices, as have been renowned for centuries, but they were arrogant, overfed and unconcerned about the poor and needy. This should be a clear warning to the Western nations regarding their treatment of the poorer nations whom they have despised and exploited.

There is much that we still need to learn about God's attitude towards human sin. There are many places in the Bible which speak about God's anger towards the nations. In Isaiah 34 God is said to be angry with 'all nations'. Through the prophet he summons them to come and listen: *"Come near, you nations, and listen; pay attention, you peoples! Let the earth hear, and all that is in it."*

There follows a long list of actions that God is going to take against the nations, but the only indication of their sins for which they are to be punished, is that his wrath is upon the armies of the nations. It is war and bloodshed that is being condemned, but in 34:8, Isaiah says *"For the Lord has a day of vengeance, a year of retribution to uphold Zion's cause"*. From this we learn that the standard of God's judgment upon the Gentile nations is their treatment of his covenant people of Israel. There are other similar statements of his anger against those who unjustly treat his people.

The Sovereignty of God

All these statements have to be seen in the light of the sovereignty of God who holds the nations in his hands as a drop in the bucket (Isaiah 40:15). All the prophets of Israel recognise the sovereignty of God that enables him to use them in working out his purposes for the nations and for his own covenant people. Jeremiah speaks about God using Babylon as the instrument of his own punishment upon the people of Judah for their sins. He even speaks of Nebuchadnezzar as his servant!

Jeremiah had been taken against his will to Egypt where he put a pile of large stones on the pavement where God told him to make a pronouncement. *"Then say this to them, 'This is what the Lord Almighty, the God of Israel, says: I will send for my servant Nebuchadnezzar king of Babylon, and I will set his throne over these stones'"* (Jer 43:10).

Calling Nebuchadnezzar his servant was not new to Jeremiah. Many years before this, Jeremiah had perceived that God not only watched over the nation of Israel, his covenant people, but he also held in his hands the destiny of each of the Gentile nations. Early in his ministry, as a young man when God called him into the prophetic ministry, God had made it clear to him that he was watching over *all the nations*, not just Judah, and that he would bring disaster from the North – code for Babylon. It was soon after the untimely death of the godly King Josiah whom Jeremiah mourned, that God revealed how he used different nations.

In Jeremiah 25 which is dated the first year of Nebuchadnezzar which would have been when he defeated the Assyrians at the Battle of Carchemish in 605 BC, God spoke to Jeremiah setting out his plans. This began with the statement that God had again and again sent prophets to the people of Israel with warning signs not to follow other gods to serve and worship them or they would put themselves outside the covenant promises of protection that Yahweh had made to the people of Israel. Then in Jeremiah 25:8 we read the dramatic statement:

*"Therefore the Lord Almighty says this: because you have not listened to my words, I will summon all the peoples of the North and **my servant Nebuchadnezzar king of Babylon**, declares the Lord, and I will bring them against this land and its inhabitants and against all the surrounding nations. I will completely destroy them and make them an object of horror and scorn, and an everlasting ruin."*

Jeremiah's bold declaration of the sovereignty of God referring to Nebuchadnezzar as God's servant must have been utterly anathema to the people of Jerusalem who had a very narrow concept of Yahweh the God of Israel. It is amazing that Jeremiah was not stoned in the streets for such a statement. But Jeremiah's teaching went with the exiles to Babylon where his letters were read; and no doubt helped to preserve the faith of the people in the testing times they were to face. It is statements like this that may have paved the way for the bold declaration of Isaiah 45 where God refers to Cyrus the pagan Persian prince as his servant – once again underlining the sovereignty of the God of Creation who holds the nations in his hands.

This was the message that Jeremiah had to carry for 40 years throughout his ministry in Jerusalem, warning the leaders and the people of the terrible destruction that would come upon them if they continued in idolatry, spurning the warnings that God had sent to them over many centuries, warning them of the consequences of spiritual adultery and not fully putting their trust in the God of their fathers.

Then God gave the following amazing revelation:

"This whole country will become a desolate wasteland, and these nations will serve the king of Babylon for 70 years. But when the 70 years are fulfilled, I will punish the king of Babylon and his nation, the land of the Babylonians, for their guilt, declares the Lord, and I will make it desolate for ever. I will bring upon that land all the things I have spoken against it, all that are written in this book and prophesied by Jeremiah against all the nations. They themselves will be enslaved by many nations and great kings; I will repay them according to their deeds and the work of their hands" (Jer 25:11-14).

Accountability

That statement by Jeremiah is probably the most significant statement of the sovereignty of God in the writings of Jeremiah. The fact that it was revealed to him right at the beginning of his ministry is remarkable. It is an incredible revelation of how God holds all the nations of the world in his hands. But is also a revelation about the nature of God, of his justice, his power and his righteous demands upon all nations. We see from this statement how God was intending to use the Babylonians to bring judgment upon his own people, the people of Judah who had broken the covenant with God. But the Babylonians were a people driven by pride, arrogance and cruelty, with utter disregard of any standards of justice in pursuit of their desire for dominion. So, they too would come under the judgment of God.

When the Babylonian army finally broke through the walls of Jerusalem in 586 BC, they carried out terrible atrocities of bloodshed – even smashing babies against brick walls, raping and murdering at will. These atrocities put them right outside the purposes of God and made them liable for the strongest possible retribution – for Babylon to be laid waste and never to be inhabited again. That judgment has been fulfilled to the letter – its ruins are still there today, but there are no inhabitants. Saddam Hussein, in the 1990s, tried rebuilding its ruins, but he never completed the task. When God makes a pronouncement of judgment of this magnitude, nothing can stand against him fulfilling his purposes.

There are many more incidents in the history of Israel and the work of their prophets which indicate the standards of behaviour that God requires of the nations in terms of their treatment of one another, of norms of behaviour that conform to godly standards of righteousness and justice. For example, we learn from Jeremiah's 'Temple Sermon' in Jeremiah 7 that God hates oppression and injustice in the same way as he hates violence, the shedding of innocent blood and immorality; and he also hates idolatry and false religion. These were the six sins of Jerusalem that required repentance if the city was to be spared from judgment. We will deal with this subject a little more fully in the next chapter.

Recent History

If we examine recent history in the light of this revelation of God's standards and if we look at the contemporary situation in the nations reflected in our daily newspapers, we have to conclude that the judgment of God upon the nations today is thoroughly deserved. In the final chapter of this book we will look at the contemporary situation in the context of the word of God that we have been examining.

The big question facing us is whether God will intervene in human history to save humanity from self-destruction. We have many times said that God does not have to mete out punishment because the sinful nature of human beings brings its own retribution. But in a world armed with nuclear weapons the consequences of human beings entering into conflict with one another on a global scale with weapons of ultimate destruction are a distinct possibility.

Isaiah, in an apocalyptic vision, foresaw human rebellion on a global scale, that would bring global destruction. He saw:

"The Earth is broken up, the Earth is split asunder, the Earth is thoroughly shaken. The Earth reels like a drunkard, it sways like a hut in the wind; so heavy upon it is the guilt of its rebellion that it falls – never to rise again" (Is 24:19-20).

Former generations of biblical scholars used to dismiss this prophecy as fantasy – in the realm of science fiction – because it was thought to be impossible. Today we know that we live in a world where unredeemed nations have their fingers on the buttons that could produce a nuclear storm. If a third world war breaks out it could fulfil Isaiah's vision. We should, therefore look more carefully at this prophecy.

The spirit of rebellion in human nature could overcome the rational knowledge of the incredible destruction that would be the inevitable outcome of a nuclear war. It could indeed shake the earth, leaving part of it an uninhabitable wilderness. The great theological question facing us now is, whether God will allow the rebellious spirit in human beings to bring the world to such a level of destruction of the natural environment. Or will the God of Creation intervene in some way?

CHAPTER 9

THE WORD OF THE LORD
TO BRITAIN

"What do you see, Jeremiah?" This was the first question God put to Jeremiah at the beginning of his ministry. He had to learn to observe carefully what was happening around him and then to spread it before the Lord for understanding. This was the essence of the prophetic ministry – it was what Jeremiah later called *"standing in the Council of the Lord"*. He even had to learn the Lord's sense of humour as he responded to that first question – *"I see the branch of an almond tree,"* he replied. And the Lord said, *"You have seen correctly, for I am watching to see that my word is fulfilled"* (Jer 1:11-12). This was a pun using the word *shaqed* ('almond') and *shoqed* ('watching').

The Purposes of God

But this was more than a mere play on words: it was a fundamental pronouncement based upon the sovereignty of God that was about to take Jeremiah into his lifelong controversy with the priests and temple authorities in Jerusalem. It was the basic statement that God, the God of Creation, who is also the God of Israel, is active in his creation and is working out his purposes towards the achievement of his end purpose – the eventual harmonisation of the whole creation including humanity, and the establishment of the Kingdom of God on earth as set out in the vision in Isaiah 2:3-5.

"Come, let us go up to the mountain of the Lord, to the house of the God of Jacob. He will teach us his ways, so that we may walk in his paths. The law will go out from Zion, the word of the Lord from Jerusalem . . ."

Human beings, driven by human rationality believe they are in control of their own destiny and everything depends upon the decisions they take. This was the problem with the priests and temple authorities who did not recognise what the prophets called *"the deeds of the Lord"*.

They certainly believed that Yahweh was present in the temple, which was his throne, and it was therefore a holy place which he would defend against all intruders. But they did not take note that God's promises were conditional upon the obedience and faithfulness of the people of Israel.

This myth of the inviolability of the temple and the city of Jerusalem was a dangerous false belief, as Jeremiah was at pains to declare. It was based upon false theology – a fundamental misunderstanding of the nature and purposes of God. The religious authorities in Jerusalem did not recognise that the God of Creation did not create the world and fling the stars into orbit and then cease all creative activity. The prophets, from Moses to Malachi, all understood this, but the religious authorities responsible for running the state religion were locked into an institutional mindset that restricted their spiritual vision.

All the prophets struggled against this basic spiritual blockage in the people. Isaiah, at his call to ministry, following an amazing experience of the presence of God in the temple, responded eagerly to God's call to ministry, but this was quickly followed by the instruction to go and tell the people:

"Be ever hearing, but never understanding; be ever seeing, but never perceiving. Make the heart of this people calloused; make their ears dull and close their eyes. Otherwise they might see with their eyes, hear with their ears, understand with their hearts and turn and be healed" (Is 6:9-10).

We have already dealt with this passage in Chapter Five, but it is essential here to recognise the nature of the spiritual blockage that existed in Jerusalem around the official institutional practice of Judaism, which has close resemblances to the institutional structures of Christianity that have been set up by the Gentile nations. We will return to the subject of this spiritual blockage in Chapter Ten, but first it is necessary to look at what Jeremiah perceived from a careful survey of the social and spiritual life of the nation.

Shaking the Nation

Arguably, the greatest speech recorded in the Bible, apart from the Sermon on the Mount, was Jeremiah's 'Temple Sermon' preached on the steps outside the temple in Jerusalem – the temple from which he was banned by the priests who hated to hear his message because their eyes and ears were closed to the truth.

Jeremiah's 'Temple Sermon' is a model declaration of the word of God applied to a contemporary situation in the history of the people of Israel. It has all the passion, power, and authority of truth flowing directly from the throne of God. The Temple Sermon occupies the whole of chapter 7, apart from verse 16, which is an editorial insertion instructing Jeremiah to cease praying for the **welfare** of the nation because that would be going contrary to the will of God.

God was not looking for opportunities of blessing the nation – *he was calling for repentance and change*. So, this was a warning to the prophet not to expect any sudden turnaround or lifting of the judgment that was coming upon the nation. It was a warning to Jeremiah not to be fainthearted, watering down the message he was declaring – it had to be a clear warning.

Three times Jeremiah was told to stop praying for the nation – because it was no use praying for God to bless a nation that was so steeped in sinful rejection of God that it was not possible for God to bless them. The only valid prayer was to ask God's assistance in bringing a spirit of repentance into the nation.

The Blessing Song

We are facing a similar situation today when there is a great need for a clear message. At the time when most nations were having their populations locked down in their homes due to the Covid 19 pandemic, millions of people across the world listened to a song purportedly conveying the blessing of God upon the people. *The Blessing* music videos took the worldwide Church by storm during the days of lockdown when many people were suffering from stress. The songs from many nations went viral across the internet. The Blessing videos were recorded in the UK – America – Canada – Hawaii - The Philippines – Zimbabwe - South Africa – Ghana – Nigeria - Sweden, and many other countries, including a Scottish Celtic Blessing recorded part in Gaelic, part in English. There was also a Hebraic version sung by one Messianic Jew.

The videos nearly all came in the same format: multiple singers and musicians recording their vocal or instrumental part individually in their own homes – and it was all skilfully mixed in a studio to produce a united, harmonious sound. In that sense the songs were a remarkable feat of achievement. The time and effort put into these recordings and their result was remarkable. They were beautiful and authentic. Surely, they must have been inspired by God? But there are good grounds for saying 'No' to that question.

The British Version

I understand from those who know Tim Hughes, who headed the UK Blessing Song project, that he is a truly humble man of God and that he was urged to undertake the task by some senior church leaders. But did anyone really ask the Lord if this was the message that he wanted to send to the nation? The Blessing Song used the Aaronic Blessing in the Bible, but it added the refrain "He is for you. He is for you." This was repeated again and again as the central part of the message. There was no mention of a call to repentance, or any conditions attached to the blessing of God that was being offered.

Of course, we all want to do something to bless others and we long to see people come into the kingdom. One of the things that Jesus said to his disciples at the Last Supper was that they should go and bear fruit – *"fruit that will last"*, which, of course meant making other disciples. He said, *"I am the vine; you are the branches. If a man remains in me and I in him he will bear much fruit."* But Jesus added, ***"Apart from me you can do nothing"*** (John 15:5).

The reason Jesus added that caution was because of our human tendency to do things in our own strength – particularly when we see an opportunity to serve the Lord and to reach others with a godly message. But Jesus had warned the disciples earlier in his ministry that he himself could do nothing on his own initiative. He said:

"I tell you the truth, the Son can do nothing by himself; he can do only what he sees his Father doing, because whatever the Father does the Son also does. For the Father loves the Son and shows him all he does" (John 5:19-20).

It should be obvious that if Jesus could do nothing on his own initiative, we ourselves should seek to do only what he tells us to do. So often, in our eagerness, we do what the Bible calls "un-commanded work", as the sons of Aaron did when they put the wrong ingredients into their censers with explosive results (Lev 10:1). However good our intentions, if we are engaged in any form of ministry and we do things on our own initiative without being under the direction of the Lord we can so easily put ourselves against God.

It is like the prophets in Jeremiah's day who were saying 'Peace, peace' when God was saying, there is no peace. In the same way if we pronounce a blessing in the name of God and God says that he is not blessing that particular situation, but calling for repentance, we actually put ourselves against God's purposes. If we are to guard against doing things in our own strength we have to learn to listen to the Lord. If we see an opportunity for doing good work, but rush ahead with great enthusiasm without consulting the Lord, we could actually be doing things against his will.

I believe that is what happened with the Blessing Song in May 2020. In *Prophecy Today UK* we published an article that expressed these concerns which caused a huge amount of controversy.[14] We cannot avoid the fact that Britain is a nation that has gone farther and farther away from biblical truth in every aspect of its national life. And this is the reason why God is shaking everything now, giving us the opportunity to pause and think about the state of the nation. The global pandemic has given an ideal opportunity for the church to be the prophet to the nation, declaring the word of God for our times. It needs to be a word that exposes what is wrong in the nation and why God is shaking everything.

Therefore, to broadcast a message saying that God is blessing each one of us is not only misleading, but it is directly against the message that God wants conveyed to the nation. However much goodwill lay behind the production of the Blessing Song, it was conveying the opposite of the word of God to the nation. God was calling for repentance and change, not saying that he was blessing a sinful nation. In the same way as Jeremiah was told three times not to pray for the welfare and blessing of God on the nation,[15] Christians who are listening to God today are hearing the same message.

Britain is under judgment and the only valid declaration that we can make in God's name is a call for repentance. We have no right to declare God's blessing on a nation that God says he is shaking; because his shaking is for a purpose; and that purpose is to bring the nation to recognise its sinfulness. If we do anything to disguise the true message of God, or to distort it, or to hide it beneath a sugar coated Blessing, we are in grave danger of putting ourselves against God, or becoming like the watchman on the wall whom Ezekiel warns to blow the trumpet or be held responsible for the coming disaster (Ezekiel 33).

---

14 "A Time for Blessing" in *Prophecy Today*, published 08.05.2020.

15 Jeremiah 7:16; 11:14 and 14:11.

Nevertheless, it was a beautiful song that blessed many Bible believing Christians at a time when they needed to hear God's blessing upon them. But it should have been accompanied by an explanation that God's blessing can only be received by those who are in right relationship with him. The song provided a wonderful opportunity to give the gospel to millions, and to speak about repentance and receiving Jesus into our lives, but it was a lost opportunity. If those behind this project had really taken time to listen to the Lord carefully, they would no doubt have heard him telling them exactly what to do, in order to use the song to bring many into the kingdom. Oh that Christians would learn to listen to the Lord!

Watchmen

The corona virus pandemic with its lockdown and enforced closure of schools and virtually the whole national economy made everyone aware that the nation is in a state of crisis. That crisis is still upon us but very few people in the nation recognise the reason why the crisis has occurred. We are a nation driven by post-modernist secular humanist concepts that prevent us from perceiving the truth. The only way the nation could hear the truth is if it is declared by Bible-believing Christians who are the moral and spiritual watchman of the nation.

In ancient Israel they had watchmen patrolling the walls of the cities to look out for any signs of danger so that they could blow a trumpet of warning to mobilise the defences of the city when they saw an enemy approaching. In moral and spiritual terms that is the role of the church as watchman, and as God used prophets to declare the word of God to the people – that is the role of the church today: but there is an **accountability** built into that role.

Ezekiel 33:6 says *"But if the watchman sees the sword coming and does not blow the trumpet to warn the people and the sword comes and takes the life of one of them, that man will be taken away because of his sin, but I will hold the watchman accountable for his blood"*. Then the word of God came to Ezekiel: *"Son of man, I have made **you** a watchman for the house of Israel, so hear the word I speak and give them warning from me."* In the same way God is saying to the church today: **"I have made you a watchman for Britain, so hear the word I speak and give them warning from me."**

This is why the Blessing Song, beautiful though it is – was the wrong message without an explanation of what God is doing today. When we give the wrong message, we are in grave danger of putting ourselves against God. We will come to the theme of what God is saying to the **church** in the next chapter, but now we will specifically ask the question, **"What is God saying to the nation of Britain?"**

First, it is essential to remember that **the word of God is not given for condemnation, but for *salvation.*** Jesus says specifically *"I did not come to judge the world, but to save it"* (John 12:47). His second coming will be to judge the nations. But his first coming into the world presents a perfect dilemma for every individual human being as well as for nations. We either accept the truth or we deny it. Jesus himself says: *"This is the verdict: light has come into the world, but men loved darkness instead of light because their deeds were evil."* (John 3:19). In his prologue, John states *"In him was life, and that life was the light of men. The light shines in the darkness, but the darkness has not understood it"* (John 1:4).

As Lesslie Newbigin says, "Jesus is, quite simply, God's revelation of himself. It is God whom we meet when we meet Jesus. To believe in him is to believe in God, because Jesus is the perfect obedient messenger of God."[16]

To believe in Jesus is to be delivered from the world of darkness, of lies and fake news and to live on a different plane. Jesus unveils a reality of truth that is hidden from those who are immersed in the world of darkness, clinging to an illusion that never satisfies. But it is not enough to believe as a matter of intellectual assent. True belief is a matter of active obedience. Just hearing the words of Jesus is not enough: we have to 'obey' them. When Jesus gave the Great Commission in Matthew 28:19-20, he did not only tell his followers to go and make disciples and teach them – but teach them to *obey* everything he had commanded them; otherwise they become like the seed trying to grow upon rocky ground and not in fertile soil.

Temple Sermon

With that in mind we return to Jeremiah's 'Temple Sermon' in which he spoke of the six sins of Jerusalem which he knew were

---

16 Lesslie Newbigin, *The Light Has Come, An Exposition of the Fourth Gospel,* Handsel Press, Edinburgh, 1982, page 165.

offensive to God. He knew that if the nation continued with these practices, they would bring the wrath of God upon themselves by causing God to remove his cover of protection over the city. This is the heart of the Temple Sermon that needs to be studied for its relevance to the situation in which we now find ourselves in 21st century Britain.

"This is what the Lord Almighty, the God of Israel, says: 'Reform your ways and your actions, and I will let you live in this place. Do not trust in deceptive words and say, "This is the temple of the Lord, the temple of the Lord, the temple of the Lord!" If you really change your ways and your actions and deal with each other justly, if you do not oppress the alien, the fatherless or the widow and do not shed innocent blood in this place, and if you do not follow other gods to your own harm, then I will let you live in this place, in the land I gave to your forefathers for ever and ever. But look, you are trusting in deceptive words that are worthless" (Jer 7:3-8).

The six sins, in the order Jeremiah gives them are: false religion, injustice, oppression, violence, idolatry and immorality. It is noteworthy that his first sin is 'false religion'. This is the charge he had been bringing against the priests in the temple since the beginning of his ministry. The scribes, who were the theologians studying the Torah, were misinterpreting the word of God and giving false teaching to the people. This was the major charge that Jeremiah brought against the religious leaders of the nation. He said, *"But my people do not know the requirements of the Lord. How can you say, we are wise, for we have the law of the Lord, when actually the lying pen of the scribes has handled it falsely?"* (Jer 8:7-8).

Jeremiah knew that once the temple authorities distorted the word of God, moving away from the truth, they were left with only worldly wisdom to guide them, which inevitably meant that they were giving wrong teaching to the people. They were, in fact, saying that Jerusalem was perfectly safe as God would never allow foreigners to enter the temple which was his holy dwelling. This meant that they were not addressing the real moral and spiritual state of the nation where there were all the usual sins of the flesh, adultery, greed and corruption, as well as the sins of idolatry, worshipping other gods and having no trust in the God of Israel.

This led to the serious charges of misleading the people; lulling them into a false sense of security, and not dealing with reality, which would lead to disaster. He said:

"From the least to the greatest all are greedy for gain, prophets and priests alike, all practice deceit. They dress the wound of my people as though it were not serious. 'Peace, peace', they say, when there is no peace" (Jer 8:10-11).

This statement is central to the message of Jeremiah that he proclaimed in the streets of Jerusalem for 40 years. There are many Bible believing Christians in Britain today who can identify with this statement. I have personally been bringing warnings for many years that unless there was repentance and a change of direction in the nation, God would shake everything – all the things that are part of our godless structure of society. Now that the time of the great shaking has arrived, we must seek revelation from God for the message that he wants delivered to the nation.

The Wrong Message

Obviously, it is no use going on warning the nation that a shaking is coming: it is here already! God's call to the nation is for repentance and turning from the way that is leading to death and disaster. Already we have seen the death of many thousands of our citizens from the coronavirus and there is no end in sight where we can say that we have completely eradicated the disease and the plague is over. Indeed, I believe God is saying that the plague and times of hardship will not end until his word is heeded.

Britain has a long heritage of biblically based Judeo-Christian teaching in its history. That is not to say that we have ever been a godly nation. There are undoubtedly some appalling blemishes in our history, such as colonial slavery for which we have never as a nation fully repented and undertaken any form of reparations. We were responsible for transporting millions of Africans across the Atlantic into a lifetime of cruel slavery in which we not only dehumanised them but we stripped them of their identity, their culture, their language, their human dignity and even their names in order to use their labour to build the economic wealth of our cities and many of our citizens.

It seems unbelievable now looking back that we could have entertained such a monstrous cruelty on which the whole nation thrived; with some two thirds of the national economy being linked to slavery in the year 1800, as mentioned earlier. The conscience of the nation has recently been stirred by the cruelty of a white policeman murdering a black man in full view of the TV cameras in Minneapolis USA. Whether or not this will lead to repentance and a change of mindset leading to attitudes of white superiority being changed, has yet to be determined. But the legacy of slavery is just one issue that still needs to be addressed in Britain.

The Plumb Line

Our centuries of biblical heritage and scholarship provided a powerful foundation for the social and personal values of the nation. These were evident in the Victorian era when moral values were strongly asserted, not only in the church but in all the institutions of the nation. Typical, was a booklet issued by the City of London giving guidance for business leaders in matters pertaining to staff relationships. It was full of biblical quotes urging upholding the highest standards of trust, truthfulness and integrity in business dealings. It was biblically based values such as these that made the City of London be seen throughout the world as a safe place for depositing their wealth and for engaging in business agreements. Tradesmen did not have to examine the small print of an agreement in minute detail. It was the boast of the City in Victorian London that the shake of a man's hand was sufficient to seal a deal that was trustworthy and honest.

Biblical values were the foundation for the values of the nation in the 19th and early 20th century, but from the rise of the pop culture in the 1960s a social revolution has taken place and, as we have seen in earlier chapters of this book, many signs have been sent warning of the danger we face, but all have been ignored.

There is plenty of evidence in the history of Israel of the consequences of ignoring the warning signs that God sends to those who are listening. Amos 7 speaks of signs of a swarm of locusts coming just at the time of the second harvest which traditionally was given to the poor. The prophet Amos interceded on behalf of the people and the threat of the plague of locusts was lifted. On another occasion there was a threat of fire sweeping across the land and once again the prophet interceded on behalf of the people. Then in a third incident Amos was shown a picture of the Lord standing by a wall with a plumb line in his hand. This time Amos refrained from pleading with God because he knew that the outrageous behaviour of the people was offensive to God and a time of judgment had come.

The little picture that Amos saw has a strong message for us today. In Israel at that time many cities were walled for the protection of their citizens and the walls were usually built with a mixture of brick and rock in two sections with the cavity between the inner and outer sections filled with rubble which was often also mixed with the rubbish from the city which in time generated heat and expanded. The task of the city engineer was to walk along the top of the walls and lower a plumb line which would show any bulging that was developing which was a sign of internal corruption. This could lead to a sudden collapse of the wall and it was the engineer's responsibility to notify the city elders of any such danger that could threaten the safety of the entire city population.

Such a possibility is reflected elsewhere in the Bible where the prophet Isaiah gives a powerful warning to the people of Jerusalem. He says:

"Because you have rejected this message, relied on oppression and depended on deceit, this sin will become for you like a high wall, cracked and bulging, that collapses suddenly in an instant. It will break in pieces like pottery, shattered so mercilessly that among its pieces not a fragment will be found for taking coals from a hearth or scooping water out of a cistern" (Is 30:12-14).

We do not depend upon coal fires or wells for our water, but the message of the high wall cracked and bulging because of inner corruption should certainly speak to us today. As we noted in Chapter Five there have been many signs in recent years. But with a biblically barren population and a spiritually inept church the warning signs have neither been interpreted nor heeded.

San Remo

Another national sin that sits alongside the atrocity of colonial slavery in terms of its monumental significance is the breaking of the sacred trust of San Remo. The vast majority of people in Britain today have probably never heard of San Remo and those who have, simply know it as a beautiful seaside resort in the Italian Riviera.

It is quite possible that many Christians and church leaders do not know that 24 April 2020 was the 100th anniversary of the signing of the San Remo international legal Agreement whereby Britain undertook the sacred duty of establishing a homeland for the Jewish people in what was then known as the land of Palestine. It was even marked out geographically as the land between the territory of Iraq and the Mediterranean Sea. This was all part of the British mandate; in 1922 the Council of the League of Nations approved a British addendum to establish the Kingdom of Transjordan on the east bank of the River Jordan, but leaving the whole of the land between the River Jordan and the Mediterranean Sea as the homeland for the Jews.

Britain not only failed to keep its word signed in the International Agreement presided over by the leaders of European states, the USA and the British Prime Minister Lloyd George and Colonial Secretary Winston Churchill. But Britain actively encouraged the Arabs, of whom there were very few in the early 20th century, to increase their occupancy of the land. At the same time Britain turned away Jewish migrants wanting to settle in the land. Britain was still carrying out this policy in 1933 to 1939 when Germany was persecuting Jews and many thousands of lives could have been saved if it had not been for British colonial policy favouring the Arabs.

Much more could be said on this subject particularly as Britain's historical anti-Semitism still directs its foreign policy with the Foreign Office routinely directing the British representative in the UN to vote against Israel every time the Arabs bring some charge against Israel before the United Nations. Britain always puts its oil interests ahead of its commitment to examine issues justly. The subject of British Foreign Office antipathy to Israel was so notorious in the 1980s that it was featured in the British comedy series 'Yes, Prime Minister' Series One, in a BBC TV programme entitled "A Victory For Democracy" where the Prime Minister wanted to support Israel in a vote at the UN, but the Foreign Office refused to countenance such an action, overriding the wishes of the Prime Minister.

British foreign policy is unchanged even today whereby Britain still refuses to recognise Jerusalem as the capital of Israel and move the British Embassy from Tel Aviv up to Jerusalem as the Americans have done with their embassy. In many other ways British anti-Semitism is displayed on the world scene as it was in Parliament until the 2019 General Election when the Parliamentary Labour Party under Jeremy Corbyn's leadership had a huge problem with anti-Semitism.

This anti-Semitism has national implications of a spiritual nature because one of the criteria by which the nations are judged in biblical terms is their attitude towards the people of Israel. In Isaiah 34 there is a call to all nations to listen and pay attention because *"The Lord is angry with all nations; his wrath is upon their armies"* (Is 34:2). The chapter is about God's judgment of the nations and a major reason is said to be their unjust treatment of his covenant people. *"For the Lord has a day of vengeance, a year of retribution, to uphold Zion's cause"* (Is 34:8).

There are many similar warnings in Scripture that indicate that systemic anti-Semitism has its roots in a hatred of God. The whole world knows that the people of Israel have a special connection with God and the spirit of rebellion in the nations today that we have noted in Chapter Eight inevitably rebounds upon Israel.

Innocent Blood

A third great sin in Britain is the shedding of innocent blood that in many places the Bible says is *"detestable to God"*. Since the passing of the Abortion Act 1967 more than 9 million babies have been torn from their mother's wombs and burnt in the incinerators linked with our hospitals and clinics. This heinous crime that is the outcome of our godless society is sufficient on its own, apart from all other crimes, to bring the wrath of God upon the nation. God's attitude to burning babies in the fire is vividly described in Jeremiah 7 where the people of Jerusalem were burning their babies in the fire on the altars of foreign gods.

God pronounced a terrible judgment upon the people of Jerusalem for burning their babies:

"So beware, the days are coming, declares the Lord, when people will no longer call it Topheth or the Valley of Ben Hinnom, but the Valley of Slaughter, for they will bury the dead in Topheth until there is no more room. Then the carcasses of this people will become food for the birds of the air and the beasts of the earth, and there will be no one to frighten them away. I will bring an end to the sounds of joy and gladness and to the voices of bride and bridegroom in the towns of Judah and the streets of Jerusalem, for the land will become desolate" (Jer 7:32-34).

God hates the shedding of innocent blood. Long before the people of Israel entered the promised land, they were warned by God to avoid the guilt of shedding innocent blood. *"You must purge from Israel the guilt of shedding innocent blood, so that it may go well with you"* (Deut 19:13). This was the instruction given to Moses along with a list of specific practices that were detestable to God the first of which was murdering helpless babies. Moses was told:

"When you enter the land the Lord your God is giving you, do not learn to imitate the detestable ways of the nations there. Let no one be found among you who sacrifices his son or daughter in the fire" (Deut 18:9-10).

All the prophets of Israel emphasise that God is a God of justice as well as a God of love and that he hates injustice and oppression. Psalm 106 gives a potted history of Israel and it records how they disobeyed the command given to Moses when they entered the land of Canaan. It says *"They mingled with the nations and adopted their customs . . . They shed innocent blood, the blood of their sons and daughters, whom they sacrificed to the idols of Canaan, and the land was desecrated by their blood"* (Ps 106:35,38).

Defiling the land by shedding innocent blood was a major reason why God brought judgment upon Israel and Judah by sending the people into exile. The record in 2 Kings 24:3 states: *"Surely these things happened to Judah according to the Lord's command, in order to remove them from his presence because of the sins of Manasseh and all he had done, including the shedding of innocent blood. For he had filled Jerusalem with innocent blood, and the Lord was not willing to forgive."*

The reckless disregard for the value of life in our society was part of the pop culture in the 1960s. The slogan "A Woman's Right To Choose" was chanted by crowds on demonstrations demanding the unfettered right of women over their own bodies in their demands for abortion. Ever since those days, the rights of the unborn child have been ignored. As a nation we have never seriously considered the demands for sexual freedom over against the right to life of the children created in a libertarian society. We have certainly never considered such matters in the context of the God of Creation who alone has the power to create life. We have the power to end it, but only God has the power to give life.

We have polluted the land with the blood of the innocent which is a grave offence in the eyes of the God of Creation. But we are part of a generation that has no knowledge of the God of the Bible. 'Extinction Rebellion' that began in 2018 with the objective of drawing attention to the dangers of polluting the natural environment leading to the extinction of many species, strongly appealed to young people and even led to schoolchildren going on strike and taking part in mass demonstrations. But with no knowledge of the God of the Bible there was no protest about the 9 million human babies that have been sacrificed to the gods of lust in Britain since the 1960s. Most people in Britain are unaware of this heinous crime.

Family Life

Back in the 1970s, when I was at London University teaching undergraduates reading for the London BSC in Sociology, one of my colleagues in the staff room handed me a copy of a small booklet entitled *Gay Liberation Front Manifesto,* London 1971. I read it with interest, but I particularly noticed towards the end of the booklet under the heading: 'The Way Forward: AIMS', it stated (page 15):

"The long-term goal of the London Gay Liberation Front, which inevitably brings us into fundamental conflict with the institutionalised sexism of this society, is to rid society of the gender role system which is at present the root of our oppression. This can only be achieved by the abolition of the family as the unit in which children are brought up."

I was aghast, not simply as a Christian, but as a sociologist. In teaching my students about structure and function in society I stressed the importance of major social institutions such as the family, the economy, education, law and government, and religion. All sociologists recognise that in terms of social processes if anyone of these five major institutions experiences a significant change, all the others are affected. The family is the key institution in the transmission of the culture from one generation to the next and in maintaining the stability of the whole socio-economic structure of society.

If family breakdown occurs on a significant scale the whole structure of society becomes unstable, particularly affecting the education of the young and the maintenance of law and order. If an organisation deliberately sets out to design activities to weaken, undermine, and destroy traditional family life they would be promoting a society heading for anarchy and chaos.

I thought at the time, these people cannot be serious. If they really mean what they say here, they are either inspired by the forces of darkness or they are utterly mad. Surely, no sane person who cares for the well-being of fellow human beings could deliberately advocate a social policy designed to destroy the family, whose knock-on effects would be to fracture every other major social institution and thereby destroy the pillars of society, eventually bringing down the whole structure of our civilisation with its Judeo-Christian foundations. But, incredible as it seemed at that time, that was their intention and it is still today.

Social Theory

It is worth pausing a moment here to see what is happening in society today in terms of social theory. Sociologists recognise five major social institutions, or areas of organised social life that are the pillars of society. These are:

(1) The Family,
(2) The Economy,
(3) Education,
(4) Law and Government,
(5) Religion.

Of course, there are many others that are influential such as **the Media, the Arts and the much-adulated NHS**, but the five major pillars have structural significance. In studying the processes of social change within these institutions, particularly in terms of structure and function, sociologists recognise the fundamental theoretical principle; namely, that where change occurs in one major social institution it produces change in each of the others.

A simple illustration of this principle may be seen in the Industrial Revolution which produced fundamental changes in the economy through changes in the means of production which affected the family by drawing people away from simple village life and rural occupations to urban complexes and industrial occupations. Education had to be formalised and thus taken out of the family. Changes in law and law-enforcement were required to meet new forms of social interaction; belief systems and values were inevitably changed through bringing together people from different cultures into close communication.

Since the early days of the rise of the pop culture in the 1960s, the whole of our Western civilisation has been experiencing a new phenomenon – the generation of forces of change within each of the major institutions of society, each of which affects the others, thereby creating a complex system of interaction never before seen and resulting in a highly volatile and unstable social situation.

In simple terms, society, as the aggregate of human beings, bears many of the characteristics of the individual personality. There is a limit to the amount of fundamental changes that each individual can experience and absorb within a given period of time without experiencing instability and insecurity, resulting in uncharacteristic behaviour, or even break down.

For example, if a person experiences marriage breakdown, loss of family through death or accident, loss of job and possibly loss of home – all in a very short space of time, it is highly likely to result in some form of breakdown. The capacity to absorb change will, of course, vary from individual to individual. This is also true for societies, but the fact remains that each society or nation does have a limit to its capacity to absorb radical changes in its major institutions without experiencing the shaking of its foundational social value system upon which the whole structure depends.

Once the value system is disturbed the whole life of the nation becomes unstable. In Britain we have experienced a series of body blows to our value system in a single decade. In 2010 David Cameron announced his Government's intention to change the definition of marriage to include homosexual relationships which dealt a fundamental blow to the institution of the family. This was followed in the middle of the decade by the critical point being reached in our relationships with the European Union resulting in the 2016 Referendum, producing a narrow decision to leave the EU which immediately affected law and government in Britain as well as the economy, but it would inevitably affect all our social institutions. The decision also divided the nation almost in half and created a high level of anxiety for the unknown future.

This was followed in 2020 by the coronavirus pandemic locking down the nation from all normal forms of human interaction including contact between the nuclear family and extended family units, forcing individuals to remain in their homes, with mounting levels of personal anxiety, due to loss of income as well as physical discomfort. There were many reports of an increased level of domestic abuse and violence including child abuse as a result of being confined to a small space and a lack of open-air activity and exercise.

Possible Outcomes

In purely sociological terms, when a situation of gross national instability occurs there are several likely outcomes.

One is the rise of a dictator in the role of socio-economic saviour such as Adolf Hitler who was accepted by the whole population of Germany to pull them out of the years of depression of the late 1920s and early 1930s.

A second possible outcome is that of a political revolution. This could occur through a group determined to overthrow the existing social order by violence as in the French Revolution of the late 18th century, or in the 1917 Bolshevik revolution in Russia. In a highly volatile situation such as we have today wherein the Judeo-Christian value system upon which the whole of Western civilisation rests, the coronavirus pandemic, followed by a severe economic crisis, complicated by a plague of locusts affecting food production in a large part of the world leading to widespread famine, the likelihood of their producing violent revolutions in different nations is quite high.

A third possibility is that of widespread economic collapse leading to hunger and famine in many parts of the world that would have social consequences in the breakdown of law and order that could overwhelm the civilian police forces and call for military intervention in the face of violence on the streets.

Another outcome is the possibility of a spiritual revival creating a radical change in the value system generated by a small group of activists who recognise the danger to society and who are genuinely inspired by supernatural power to communicate the word of God into society.

The Welsh revival of 1906 is an illustration of the radical change that can occur in a nation when the spirit of God transforms individuals which spills over among their friends and neighbours and spreads rapidly to affect wider society around them. In an age of mass communication such as we have today with social media at the fingertips of multitudes, it is quite possible for a spiritual revival to spread rapidly in a time of crisis.

It is interesting for me to be writing this, which is very similar to the different outcomes that I was seeing in the late 1970s when I wrote the book *Towards the Dawn*. The three different outcomes I saw then were, political rebellion, spiritual revival, or a social revolution. Political revolution was very much in the air at that time with widespread unemployment, industrial strife and strikes compounded by fears of war. Spiritual revival was also very much in the expectation of many Christians as the Charismatic Movement was gaining strength. Thirdly, the rise of post-modernist secular humanism was high on the agenda for an increasing number of social groups.

In the analysis that I offered in *Towards the Dawn*, I concluded that the most likely way forward was the advance of post-modernism shaking the foundations of our society. In the event, that has proved to be the way society has moved in the past 40 years, and we need now to take stock of the present situation in order to see the way ahead. Clearly we are at a crossroads in terms of social change and if we are not to lose the whole of our Judeo-Christian heritage in either a violent political revolution, or a secular humanist social revolution, we must rightly evaluate the situation in order to map the way ahead.

Revolutionary Movements

The Gay Liberation group of the early 1970s has morphed into the LGBT+ movement of today that spans the world. It has achieved huge political influence in most Western nations. In Britain it has infiltrated all the political parties and is particularly influential among civil servants in Whitehall and in the staff and management of the BBC. Hence its influence is strong both in government and in the media, with the power to sway public opinion and to guide legislation. It even has a strong link into the 'Black Lives Matter' movement that sprang into worldwide public attention in May 2020 with the widely televised news coverage of the George Floyd incident in the USA. The demonstrations that followed, and the tearing down of colonial statues escalated across the world, especially affected Western nations.

The confluence of the LGBT+ movement with the 'Extinction Revolution' climate change movement and the 'Black Lives Matter' movement is highly significant. All of them have an anti-Judeo-Christian biblical basis as well as being anti-Semitic.

Their objective is to undermine biblical values that are at the heart of Western civilisation. The grave danger facing all those who value our Judeo-Christian heritage is that the vast majority of people do not recognise the true objectives of these three movements and the threat that they represent.

Research

I have been working in public life throughout the past 40 years with high-level contacts in the political, social and religious sectors of society in Britain. I have been able to observe at close quarters the forces of change in our society, how they have developed and how they have been handled by leading politicians and churchmen. Throughout that time, I have been responsible for, or involved in, the publication of academic research drawing attention to the dangers of the changes taking place in society, but time after time these dangers have been quietly side-lined or openly ignored.

In 1983 I led the research team that produced the Parliamentary Enquiry into 'video nasties', showing the effect of violent video films upon children. Further reports on the family followed in 1996, 1998 and in the 2000s through the Lords and Commons Family and Child Protection Group of which I was convener for 25 years. The group works in teams of working parties investigating different issues affecting the health and welfare of children and families.

One of the teams led by Dr Lisa Noland carried out research into the activities and influence of homosexual groups. They produced reports on the potential threat to the health of the nation of an alarming nature. The levels of violent sexual activity involving different forms of anal sex is something of which most people in the general public are totally unaware, especially the threat to health for young men as the anal passage in human beings is not designed for such perversions that cause bleeding, allowing human waste product into the blood circulation, leading to disease and death. Young men should be warned that when they enter the world of homosexual practices, they are reducing their life expectancy by some 30 years. They are also subject to a range of sexually transmitted diseases which, especially if they are bisexual, can spread rapidly in society.

These practices are not new to the 20th and 21st centuries, in fact they stretch back thousands of years and are roundly condemned in the Bible. But we have a whole generation of young people today who have little or no knowledge of the Bible, so they have probably never heard of Sodom and Gomorrah, towns that were destroyed for engaging in the very practices that are now promoted and celebrated by the LGBT+ movement.

The Sins of the Amorites

We took a brief look at the Amorites in Chapter 2, but due to the significance for today of the type of sins they practised, we are returning to the subject here to go into a little more depth.

The group practising the most extreme form of violent sexual aberrations to come under the condemnation of God were the Amorites. They originated from the area around Babylon in what is now Iraq and moved to the land of the Canaanites, which we now know as Israel, somewhere between 3000 and 2500 BC. They mixed and intermarried with the Canaanites and other groups in the period between the time when Abraham and Sarah lived on the land, and the settlement of the people of Israel in the time of Joshua.

During that time Abraham's family became 'the people of Israel' who spent some 400 years in Egypt. Then, after their departure from Egypt they spent a further 40 years in the desert under the leadership of Moses before crossing the Jordan, led by Joshua and entering the land of Canaan. Moses had prepared the people carefully for entering the land by giving them the teaching that he had received from God. He also tried to guard them against losing their identity by intermarrying with the foreign tribes now occupying the land of Canaan which many generations earlier had been promised to Abraham. Moses said:

"When the Lord your God brings you into the land you are entering to possess and drives out before you many nations – the Hittites, Girgashites, Amorites, Canaanites, Perizzites, Hivites, and Jebusites, seven nations larger and stronger than you – and when the Lord your God has delivered them over to you and you have defeated them, then you must destroy them totally" (Deut 7:1-2).

From the standpoint of our 21st century culture this sounds a horrendous statement of intent. In fact, it was immediately modified by Moses telling them that they would, in fact, not have to fight against all these people, but that God would drive them out *"little by little"* (Deut 7:22). He would do that in various ways, even by sending 'the hornet' among them. God, of course, knew that the people of Israel were going to have great need of the local people – particularly the Canaanites with their agricultural skills to help them in the early years of the settlement, and the Philistines with their technological skills, as the Israelites themselves were mainly sheep and goat farmers.

The Israelites were evidently quite slow in developing all the necessary agricultural skills as several hundred years later, in the time of Saul and Jonathan, it is reported that *"Not a blacksmith could be found in the whole land of Israel, because the Philistines had said, 'Otherwise the Hebrews will make swords and spears!' So all Israel went down to the Philistines to have their ploughshares, mattocks, axes and sickles sharpened"* (1 Sam 13:19-20).

Archaeological evidence shows that the land was very sparsely occupied at the time of the settlement under Joshua, so the Hebrews were able to settle among the existing people groups who were evidently in small clusters scattered around the land. The one group whom the Israelites were specifically told to avoid or destroy were the Amorites and this was due to their religious and social practices that were said to be detestable to God. These practices not only included infant sacrifice, but also violent anal rape as described in Genesis 19:5.

During Abraham's time of living in the land of Canaan he was told by God that his descendants would go through a period of enslavement for 400 years but when they were released they would come back to this land because *"the sin of the Amorites has not yet reached its full measure"* (Gen 15:16). In due time the Israelites would come back to occupy the land and cleanse it from the pollution of the sins of shedding the blood of the innocent and of the violent sexual perversions of the Amorites.

It is the statement that ***"the sin of the Amorites has not yet reached its full measure"*** that is of particular interest for us in understanding what God is saying to Britain at this present time. If we look at this statement in the context of Paul's pronouncement on the same subject in Romans 1:18-32 we see that he identifies stages in the corruption of a society which begin with suppressing the truth of the God of Creation. Paul believes that human beings are without excuse because God's divine nature is clearly to be seen in his creation. But they turned to idolatry and then to sexual perversion; finally reaching the point where – *"They have become filled with every kind of wickedness, evil, greed and depravity. They are full of envy, murder, strife, deceit and malice . . . They invent ways of doing evil . . ."* This is the level of brutal depravity that is represented in the 'sins of the Amorites'.

It is at this point when judgment becomes inevitable because human beings are actually disturbing the fundamental principles of God's act of creation, whereby he created human beings in his own image and laid down the means of their procreation, within the family for the protection and rearing of the next generation. Homosexual practices are not only the lustful misuse of the means of procreation, but they lead to disease and death not to the joyful celebration of new life. The sins of the Amorites involved violent anal rape and bestiality. It also involved the shedding of innocent blood by sacrificing infants to their idolatrous gods in which they were driven by a spirit of death. These practices which are said to be detestable to God are so outrageous that for the sake of preserving humanity, God must intervene.

The Tipping Point

The question we are facing is this: Has Britain reached that tipping point where the sin of the Amorites, which is being practised in Britain today, reached the full measure when judgment becomes inevitable? Until the year 2010 the statistics of those actively involved in homosexual practices was very small – reportedly only 1½% / 2% of the population. But since that time there has been a major change in the nation, not only with the escalation of gay pride demonstrations, publicly celebrating their depravity, but government policy has changed.

Margaret Thatcher's Government passed a regulation in The Local Government Act known as Clause 28 that was hated by the far left and was the object of particular bitterness from post-modernist groups. It prohibited the promotion of homosexual teaching in schools and forbade literature designed to normalise homosexual family types such as the book for primary age children entitled *"Jenny lives with Eric and Martin"* which was reported in 1983 to be in primary school libraries under the Inner London Education Authority. The book was about a little girl who lived with her father and his male partner, seeking to steer primary age children away from the marriage-based family as the ideal. Margaret Thatcher personally condemned the book. But one of the first acts of the Blair Government elected in 1997 was to repeal Clause 28 giving a green light to the LGBT movement to move into achieving their objective of creating equality between heterosexual and homosexual family groups and lifestyles as being 'the new normal'.

From that time education policy rapidly changed to favour LGBT objectives with the civil servants in the Ministry of Education being particularly sympathetic and displaying their rainbow sign in the entrance hall in Whitehall. The indoctrination of children to accept homosexuality and gender change from the earliest possible age in primary schools is now public policy endorsed by all the main political parties. The harm being done to children is incalculable and the results can be seen in the increasing number of schoolchildren seeking to change their gender and others displaying symptoms of depression and mental health disorders.

Far from protecting our children in the nation's schools by teaching them the truth that faithful married couples represent the ideal family and the best environment for raising children, we actually promote the fake news and lies of a cultural Marxist society, saying that all family types are equal. The minds of the nation's children are being deliberately poisoned by the propaganda of death through the promotion of homosexual practices. This is the modern form of institutionalised child abuse, endorsed by politicians of all the major parties that needs to be changed if future generations of the nation's children are to have any chance of healthy lifestyles.

As we can see from the review of legislation in Chapter Seven and from the issues discussed in this chapter there is plenty of justification for the wrath of God to be poured out upon Britain. If we only take just two issues we can see that justification – the pollution of the land by the shedding of innocent blood through the vast number of babies we have murdered since the Abortion Act of 1967: and the legalised child abuse being carried out under our education system in the nation's schools by the indoctrination of children into lifestyles that lead to disease and death that come directly from the powers of darkness.

The Worldwide Shaking

The coronavirus pandemic is just the curtain raiser of God's judgment upon the nation. The great shaking of the nations has begun. It is not just Britain that is being shaken: the shaking is worldwide, involving all nations. In Britain we have had 40 years of warnings which have been ignored by both church and state. Now the great shaking of all the institutions in which we have invested our hopes and dreams of a just and prosperous society based upon cultural Marxism and our warped values of equality and tolerance are all collapsing around us as God begins violently to shake everything in our post-modernist society that is founded upon sand and will eventually collapse.

When God shakes a society, he shakes it very thoroughly. In Amos 9:9 God says: *"I will shake the house of Israel among all the nations as grain is shaken in a sieve, and not a pebble will reach the ground."* Only the pure grain will go through the sieve and all the pebbles will be removed. This is the purpose of shaking: to separate the good from the bad.

Today, the shaking of the nations is worldwide with the convergence of three international calamities – the coronavirus pandemic, the international financial crisis and the greatest plague of locusts ever known. There is no cure for the pandemic: it cannot be stopped; it can only be contained by people being inoculated against it or building up a resistance to it and providing a vaccine for the whole population of the world is a daunting prospect.

The knock-on effect of the financial crisis with its disruption to the economies of all nations is going to have a profound effect upon the lifestyles of millions of people. And the plague of locusts that began in the desert areas in the Middle East then spread to Asia and Africa destroying harvests that were expected to be abundant due to earlier heavy rainfall, created long term problems for millions of people. Many developing nations are facing famine and starvation at a time when the industrialised nations are struggling to feed vast numbers of unemployed; and all this is in the context of the continuing pandemic that may last for a number of years.

Interpreting the Word

If we are right in our understanding of the nature of God and his sovereignty as revealed in the Bible, there is an obligation upon those nations that embrace the Christian faith to interpret the word of God to the nations of the world, enabling them to understand what is happening and what is required of them. It was ignorance of the *"requirements of the Lord"* that Jeremiah had to face with the people of Judah. He asked: *"Since they have rejected the word of the Lord, what kind of wisdom do they have?"* (Jer 8:9). He knew that the kind of wisdom needed for an understanding of the nature and purposes of God, such as we need today, could only come from knowing the word of God.

This puts an obligation upon those nations that have had access to the word of God in the Bible for centuries, to be the prophets to the world – enabling them to understand what is happening and what is required of them. This puts an additional pressure upon nations such as Britain and America who have acknowledged the God of the Bible in the social foundations of their nations. Britain has done this through the oath sworn by the monarchs at their coronation, and America has even acknowledged God on the dollar notes of their currency – *"In God we Trust"*.

The first requirements for the Christian nations of the West has to be repentance; not only for what we have done in allowing the forces of darkness to make inroads into the culture of the nation and to corrupt the minds of children, but for the influence we have had in transmitting our corrupt values around the world – especially in linking cultural values to the giving of aid to nations dependent upon our help.

Three Strands of Judgement

The advent of the three strands of judgment – disease, economic hardship, and plague – marks the beginning of a new phase in the history of the world. The summit of God's self-revelation of his nature and purposes was reached in the advent of Jesus on the world stage. Of that advent he said: *"This is the verdict: light has come into the world, but men loved darkness instead of light because their deeds were evil."* Jesus added: *"But whoever lives by the truth comes into the light, so that it may be seen plainly that what he has done has been done through God"* (John 3:19-21).

Battle Lines

We are witnessing a heightening of the battle between the forces of light and darkness. We do not know whether this is the final great spiritual battle because all those timings are in the hands of God. Jesus told his disciples *"It is not for you to know the times or dates the Father has set by his own authority"* (Acts 1:7). But all those who watch what is happening on the international scene and within their own nation can see the increasing rate of change and the inevitable tensions that brings into society, especially in terms of human relationships, conflict and mental health problems.

On the world scene we see the persecution of Christians on a scale never before known, especially in areas of conflict with Islam, but also in China where the Communist authorities are tightening their grip upon Christians especially those in the unregistered churches who they perceive as a threat to their authoritarian Marxist regime.

A similar route of atheistic cultural Marxism is gaining power in the Western nations as the battle for the hearts and minds of children who represent the next generation becomes more intense. At the moment that battle is being fought within the state educational system, which is what we are seeing in Britain where LGBT+ teaching is becoming increasingly aggressive, and the efforts of parents to protect their children from RSE lessons are being resisted. The battleground around gender is a direct threat to the biblical concept of family and is aimed at attacking the central concept of the God of Creation who created human beings as male and female.

Great Deception of 'Equality'

On the legal side the attack upon the Judeo-Christian heritage of the nation, its cultural roots in faithful loving heterosexual marriage, and its social foundations in the structural values of society, have been concentrated upon the great deception of so-called 'equality' that has been used to strike at the heart of family life to justify same-sex marriage.

Alongside the movement for equality and justice has gone the demand for the removal of all forms of dissent from the values of cultural Marxism. So we have seen the boycotting of speakers in universities who may be perceived as offering a critique of Marxist values. We have seen the rapid rise of anarchist movements under the umbrella of climate change that gave us 'Extinction Rebellion' and the movement against racism that gave us 'Black Lives Matter' which from its inception was mixed in with LGBT values, and anarchist groups moved in to create violence and destruction on city streets.

Creating Chaos

The objectives of the anarchists are to create chaos in society so that they may slip their objectives into the mix. But alongside the anarchists are another group who are equally eager to see a chaotic state of social breakdown among the nations from which to advance their ambitions. This is the World Economic Forum who in June 2020, in the midst of the lockdown period affecting most nations, announced what they termed 'The Great Reset' aimed at resetting the economic and social systems of the world at the end of the pandemic.

They were planning a great resetting of the economic and social systems of the nations to prioritise sustainable development of the planet. Their objectives are for 'One World Government' and control of the global banking and financial investment services. Prince Charles spoke warmly of their objectives at the launch of the 'Great Reset' in May 2020, hailing it as an opportunity to reset humanity's relationship with nature. Their objectives look suspiciously like those described in the Book of Revelation where a one-world-government takes control of everything including the economy, and what we can buy and sell.

Culture War

The next stage in the battle between the forces of darkness and the forces of light will be an intensification of the culture war. The suppression of so-called 'hate speech' provides the perfect platform from which to turn upon Christianity. It is but a short step to apply this to Christians and to declare the Bible, or parts of the Bible, to be akin to racist literature. At that point the full weight of persecution of Bible believing Christians will begin.

If what we foresee as the intensification of the battle between the forces of darkness and light progresses in the near future as all the indicators show, it will be essential for Bible believing Christians to have the same quality of personal relationship with God as the Christians in the Early Church facing the cruel persecution of the Roman Empire. It may be that churches in the Western nations may have to go underground in a similar way to Christians in China in order to preserve the faith for the next generation.

But what kind of church will be needed to withstand the kind of onslaught that is just over the horizon? This is what we will examine in the next chapter.

CHAPTER 10

THE WORD OF THE LORD
TO HIS CHURCH

We have deliberately headed this chapter "The word of the Lord to *HIS* church", which requires us to say what we mean by the word 'church'. It is unfortunate that we only have the one word 'Church' with such a variety of meanings – from the global institutions of the Roman Catholic and Anglican Churches, the Protestant Free Church denominations, the 'New Churches' arising out of the 1970s Charismatic Movement, to village chapels, or independent groups of believers meeting in each other's homes.

It is well known that the scholars preparing the translation of the Authorised Version could not agree on whether the word *ecclesia* should be translated by its literal meaning 'an assembly', or follow the Roman Catholic Vulgate and use the word 'church'. They consulted King James I who had ordered the English translation and he ruled in favour of 'church'. So, we have been stuck with its ambiguity since that time.

The Greek word *ecclesia* also carries a sense of purpose. So in the New Testament we not only find it used for the gatherings of Christians, but it is also found in Acts 19:32 describing the assembly of craftsmen called by silversmith Demetrius with the purpose of murdering Paul who was a threat to their economic prosperity. The Christians, of course, gathered with the purpose of worshipping God and fulfilling the Great Commission. They were not just groups of people drawn together through a common interest, but with a common purpose. That purpose was to share with others the life-changing experience of the lordship of the Risen Christ in their lives.

Closed Churches

The coronavirus pandemic that closed churches throughout the world gave us an opportunity for reviewing not only the purpose of these buildings, and of the institutions behind them, but more fundamentally, the nature and purpose of the true 'ecclesia' as a community of believers under the headship of Jesus.

Christians throughout the world are still asking why their churches should have been closed, and more importantly, what will the church be like when the world crisis is all over. It is of foremost importance that Christians recognise the hand of God in what is happening. Just as God sent a message through Jeremiah to the people of Judah who had been taken from Jerusalem into exile in Babylon that began: *"This is what the Lord Almighty, the God of Israel, says to **all those I carried into exile** from Jerusalem to Babylon"* – in the same way God is saying to Christians today: "This is what the Lord Almighty, the God of Israel, says to **all those whose churches I closed."**

It is God who closed the churches – not the Governments of the nations!

Many will dispute that statement, but it is unarguable that God **allowed** it to happen. The biblical prophets made no distinction between the direct will of God and his allowable will – as far as they were concerned it was all one and the same thing. It was all part of the sovereignty of God. We are taking the same view here.

There are important truths that we can learn from the exile in Babylon which will help us in looking at the reasons why God allowed the churches in Britain to close. So we will spend a short time looking at the 6th century BC exile.[17]

The people of Judah had to understand that God had not only allowed the Babylonians to conquer Jerusalem, but there was a purpose in sending 10,000 people to Babylon. They had to learn the lesson of why God had allowed what seemed to them to be a catastrophic tragedy. It was not caused by the Babylonian army being more powerful than the army of Judah. It was God himself who brought this tragedy upon his people. In the same way it was God

---

17 For further understanding of the reasons why God took many people from Judah to Babylon and his purpose in bringing a redeemed community back to prepare the way for Messiah – see Clifford and Monica Hill, *Living in Babylon*, Handsel Press, Edinburgh, 2016.

who closed the churches to make us stop and consider the reasons why this should happen.

The Purpose of the Exile

When the Babylonian army departed taking with them their hostages, Jeremiah saw two baskets of figs in front of the temple. One basket had very good figs and the other overripe bad fruit, and he was told that the good figs represented those who had gone to Babylon in exile. It was God's purpose to carry out some important changes through the exile.

The first purpose was to separate the people from the **idolatry** that was being practised in Jerusalem.

"Do you not see what they are doing in the towns of Judah and in the streets of Jerusalem! The children gather wood, the fathers light the fire, and the women knead the dough and make cakes of bread for the Queen of Heaven" (Jer 7:17-18).

The second purpose of the exile was to separate the people from the **false religion** of the temple where the priests taught theology that was not in line with the word of God. They taught the people that God would not allow any foreigners to enter the city of Jerusalem or the temple because the temple was the throne of God and the city of Jerusalem was a holy city. They were relying upon false teaching on the covenant promises of God to the people of Israel. They had lost sight of the true revelation of God that had been given to the fathers of the nation and their prophets over the centuries from the time of Abraham.

God had revealed himself to be **a God of justice** as well as of love and compassion. His covenant promises were **dependent upon the obedience and trust of the people.** This was not being taught by the religious leaders of the nation in the time of Jeremiah. Hence his explosive words:

"Will you steal and murder, commit adultery and perjury, burn incense to Baal and follow other gods you have not known, and then come and stand before me in this house, which bears my name, and say, "We are safe" – safe to do all these detestable things? Has this house, which bears my name, become a den of robbers to you? But I have been watching! declares the Lord" (Jer 7:9-11).

The third purpose why God had taken many of his people into exile in Babylon was to separate them from the **government led by ungodly kings**. Since the death of Josiah there had been a succession of kings who had no respect for the word of God. Zedekiah, the last King of Judah ever to sit on the throne in Jerusalem,[18] was the worst of all. He not only led a corrupt government, but he swore an oath of fealty to Nebuchadnezzar in the name of the God of Israel which he promptly revoked, entering a conspiracy with neighbouring nations to revolt against Babylon. This brought terrible retribution upon the people including his own family.

Zedekiah's Treachery

The city of Jerusalem would never have been destroyed if it had not been for Zedekiah's treachery and stupidity in causing Jerusalem to be locked into more than two years of siege that brought starvation upon the people prior to the most fearful slaughter once the Babylonian army broke through the city walls.

The people in exile had to learn to put their trust in the government of God and not the government of human beings. From the time of Moses, they had been a nation in a covenant relationship with God that separated them from other nations. In spiritual terms they were to be separate from the world. It had never been God's intention for them to have a king. The prophet Samuel had resisted the clamour for a king, but the people had persuaded him that it was necessary for their protection. In Babylon Ezekiel faced the same problem

"You say, 'We want to be like the nations, like the peoples of the world, who serve wood and stone'. But what you have in mind will never happen. As surely as I live, declares the Sovereign Lord, I will rule over you with a mighty hand and an outstretched arm and with outpoured wrath" (Ezek 20:32-33).

Separation from the World

The people of Israel had been set aside from all the other nations in the world for a purpose. That purpose was to use them to reveal to the world God's nature and purposes and his way of salvation. Moses caught a glimpse of God's purpose when he told the people:

---

18   King Herod who was on the throne at the time of Jesus was not a pure-bred Jew and he was appointed by Rome, not elected by the people of Israel.

"The Lord did not set his affection on you and choose you because you were more numerous than other people, for you were the fewest of all peoples. But it was because the Lord loved you and kept the oath he swore to your forefathers that he brought you out with a mighty hand and redeemed you from the land of slavery, from the power of Pharaoh king of Egypt. Know therefore that the Lord your God is God; he is the faithful God, keeping his covenant of love to a thousand generations of those who love him and keep his commands" (Deut 7:7-9).

This is a statement of great significance which was understood by the prophets of Israel, but rarely understood by their leaders, either political or religious. And this became a major reason why the exile had to take place whereby a remnant was separated from the institutional structures of Israel into an environment dominated by the gross idolatries and cruel practices of Babylon. They would be a people who had to learn how to live in an idolatrous world and be spiritually separated from that world.

Ezekiel had to deal with deviance with great firmness in order to keep the people from idolatry in Babylon. *"Will you defile yourselves the way your fathers did and lust after their vile images? . . . As surely as I live, declares the Sovereign Lord, I will not let you enquire of me"* (Ezek 20:30-31). They had to learn how to identify with the holiness of God – his separation from the world.

The whole period of the exile in Babylon was to prepare a redeemed people separated from the world, purified from the sins of idolatry and the gross sins of Babylon. They were to be people who no longer relied upon the government of kings or the great institution of the temple with its animal sacrificial system which had been fiercely condemned two centuries earlier by prophets such as Isaiah of Jerusalem: *"The multitude of your sacrifices – what are they to me? Says the Lord. I have more than enough of burnt offerings, of rams and the fat of fattened animals; I have no pleasure in the blood of bulls and lambs and goats. When you appear before me, who has asked this of you, this trampling of my courts? Stop bringing meaningless offerings!"* (Is 1:11-13).

In a similar vein God had said to Hosea: *"I desire mercy, not sacrifice and acknowledgement of God rather than burnt offerings"* (Hos 6:6). And the Psalmist had said *"You do not delight in sacrifice, or I would bring it; you do not take pleasure in burnt offerings. The sacrifices of God are a broken spirit and contrite heart"* (Ps 51:16-17).

The Purposes of God

Ezekiel had prepared the way during the early years of the exile for the great revelation of his successor – Isaiah of the exile – whose passion can be seen in what is probably the longest sentence recorded in the Bible:

"This is what the Lord says – your Redeemer, who formed you in the womb: I am the Lord, who made all things, who alone stretched out the heavens, who spread out the earth by myself, who foils the signs of false prophets and makes fools of diviners, who overthrows the learning of the wise and turns it into nonsense, who carries out the words of his servants and fulfils the predictions of his messengers, who says of Jerusalem, it shall be inhabited, of the towns of Judah, they shall be rebuilt, and of their ruins, I will restore them, who says to the watery deep, 'Be dry', and I will dry up your streams, who says of Cyrus, he is my Shepherd and I will accomplish all I please; he will say of Jerusalem, let it be rebuilt, and of the temple, let its foundations be laid" (Is 44:24-28).

This great declaration to the people of Israel in exile was intended to prepare them to receive the revelation of the purposes of God - that he would use them to reveal to the world the message of his salvation:

"Turn to me and be saved, all you ends of the earth; for I am God, and there is no other. By myself I have sworn, my mouth has uttered in all integrity a word that will not be revoked: before me, every knee will bow; by me, every tongue will swear. They will say of me, in the Lord alone are righteousness and strength. All who have raged against him will come to him and be put to shame" (Is 45:22-24).

Missionary Purpose

This was the missionary purpose of God for the people of Israel that was revealed to those in exile in preparation for returning to rebuild Jerusalem and rebuild the temple in the heart of the city. God's purpose was not simply to restore the tribes of Jacob and bring back those of Israel to the land. He said, *"I will also make you a light for the Gentiles, that you may bring my salvation to the ends of the earth"* (Is 49:6).

The redeemed remnant would rebuild the temple, but it would not be like the old temple. The new temple would be *"a house of prayer for all nations"* (Is 56:7). Foreigners would be welcome within its walls if they bind themselves to the Lord to serve him, to love his name and to worship him and to keep his sabbaths. This was revolutionary for the people of Israel, but it was preparing the way for the Messianic Age when Messiah would come who would change everything by fulfilling and finalising in himself the revelation of God.

Lessons from Babylon

There were many things learned by the Jews in exile in Babylon. The following is a brief summary:[19]

- They themselves were responsible for the situation that had come upon the nation
- They did not need the temple and the priests to enable them to communicate with God
- They could pray to God in a hostile spiritual environment
- Each individual was held by God to be responsible for their faith and conduct
- The family was the primary place for the communication and preservation of the faith
- The word of God was essential for teaching and understanding the faith
- A community of believers was a God-given spiritual institution
- A building was not essential, but it was useful as a local gathering place for believers – hence the birth of the synagogue in Babylon

These are all things from which the Christians in the Early Church benefited, and which have significance for us today, in days when we are facing increasing restrictions upon our freedom to declare the word of God in public.

A Post-Crisis Church

What will the church be like after the worldwide crisis? What sort of changes is God seeking for his church? This is the question

---

19 This is drawn from our study of the 6th century BC exile in Babylon. See Clifford and Monica Hill, *Living Victoriously in Babylon, A Workbook for Study Groups*, Issachar Ministries, Sandy, 2017.

that all church leaders – and indeed all believers should be asking and urgently seeking the Lord for answers. It is his church which he has entrusted into our human hands – but what does he want to see in the post-crisis church?

If we accept the revelation of God in the Bible that shows his sovereignty, then we must accept that at least **he allowed** the churches to be closed right across the world. We should also be able to accept that this was an opportunity to rethink the whole message and purpose of the church which has, to a large extent, become married to the world in the 21st century.

We could give masses of evidence to support that statement that the church has married the world; but this is not the place to do that. We will simply make the statement that is obvious to everyone who reads the daily newspapers that the churches have become entangled in all the controversies of our changing culture and have embraced within their leadership and membership the physical and the spiritual adulteries of the world – but their leaders rarely take an unequivocal public stand upon biblical truth or the gospel.

The central problem for the church is the message of the cross of Jesus that it has to convey to the world. For the Jew the cross is scandalous and for the Greek it is absurd. The decision-point for Jesus was reached at the end of his public ministry following his triumphal entry into Jerusalem riding on the colt of a donkey (John 12:15) which would have had great significance for his disciples who knew the teaching of the *Torah* that the donkey was the only animal that had to be *"redeemed by a lamb"* before it could be used – otherwise its neck was to be broken (Ex 34:20). Why did Jesus take an unredeemed colt? Here was the Lamb of God redeeming the colt on his way to the cross where he would give his life for the redemption of the world. The symbolism was enormous!

At that point, some Greeks who had come to Jerusalem seeking God, spoke to Philip who had a Greek name, asking to meet their master. Jesus immediately saw the significance of these Gentiles coming to seek God. He said: *"The hour has come for the Son of man to be glorified"* and then he began to speak of his death. *"I tell you the truth, unless a grain of wheat falls to the ground and dies, it remains only a single seed. But if it dies, it produces many seeds"* (John 12:24).

Point of Decision

Jesus himself had to face the decision which deeply troubled him *"What shall I say? Father save me from this hour? No, it was for this very reason I came to this hour. Father, glorify your name!"* (John 12:27-28). This was the point of decision and it was at this point also that Jesus said, *"Whoever serves me must follow me"* (John 12:25).

John also records that the leaders in Jerusalem still did not believe:

"Even after Jesus had done all these miraculous signs in their presence, they still would not believe in him". He quotes the words of Isaiah 6:10, *"He has blinded their eyes and deadened their hearts, so that they can neither see with their eyes nor understand with their hearts, nor turn – and I would heal them."*

John immediately follows this with the statement: *"Yet at the same time many even among the leaders believed in him. But because of the Pharisees they would not confess their faith for fear that they will be put out of the synagogue, for they loved praise from men more than praise from God"* (John 12:42-43). **This statement is of great significance for us today**.

Why did the churches close?

The shutdown should have conveyed a strong message to Christians – especially those who are in leadership positions. Are we like the leaders in the time of Jesus who believed in him, but could not extricate themselves from the structures of the religious system in which they were involved?

The truth of God cannot be encased in a structure controlled by human beings who set the parameters of wisdom in accordance with the prevailing standards of the world. This was what confronted Jeremiah at his call to ministry when God told him that his task was *"to uproot and tear down, to destroy and overthrow, to build and to plant"* (Jer 1:10). It would not be possible to bring truth into a system controlled by worldly wisdom and driven by the forces of corruption. There had to be uprooting and tearing down, destroying and overthrowing before there could be building up and planting.

This was the point that Jesus reached at the end of his earthly ministry – unless a grain of wheat falls into the ground and dies – there has to be a breaking down before there can be a building up, a dying and a new birth. In the end it is only through a new birth that revelation of truth can be received.

This was the message of Jesus to Nicodemus who came to him by night seeking truth. But he was still firmly embedded in the religious system of the day; so Jesus told him, *"I tell you the truth, no one can see the kingdom of God unless he is born again"* (John 3:3).

I believe that through the closure of the churches in 2020 God was posing a direct question to all those who have leadership responsibilities in the churches and all those who have membership of the churches and who regularly attend their services. The question is: Is your trust solely in Jesus as Lord and Saviour above all other loyalties or are you dependent upon an institution called the 'church'? What did you learn through the period of lockdown? Of course, you missed the fellowship of other believers and collective worship, but has your relationship with God deepened in the same way as the people of Jerusalem learned to trust God in Babylon without having the temple? God is looking for a people whose trust is in him and not in the structures of institutions.

Following Jesus

The disciples had to learn that there had to be a death to self and to human institutions before there could be rebirth to glory. And this is the message of Jesus to his church today. Jesus cannot say *"Follow me"* to his church until his church understands what it means to follow him. This was the problem that confronted Peter who declared, *"Even if all fall away, I will not"* (Mark 14:29) and Jesus had to tell him that before the night was out Peter would deny him three times.

Then on one of the resurrection appearances on the beach beside the Sea of Galilee Jesus gave Peter the opportunity of reaffirming his love. He addressed him by the name he had before Jesus had renamed him 'Peter', because, far from being the 'rock', his discipleship had been built on sand. So Jesus said:

"Simon son of John, do you truly love me?" After the third time of asking, cancelling out his denials, Jesus finally said the words that meant so much to Peter, ***"Follow me!"*** Jesus had said to Peter at the Last Supper *"You cannot follow me now, but you will follow later"* (John 13:36). Peter now knew what following Jesus meant.

The great question confronting us today is: "Do we know what following Jesus means in this 21st century world?" Are we prepared to lay down our church structures at the foot of the cross and ask Jesus to rebuild his church that has become corrupted by marrying the world? Are we prepared for the tearing down of things in our own lives before the building up?

Jeremiah was told that there had to be tearing down before there could be building up; and Jesus said the grain of wheat had to fall into the ground and die before there could be new life. The old corrupt structures have to be torn down before there can be new life. You cannot put new wine into old wine skins. We all know the teaching of Jesus, but we are afraid to apply it to our own situation. Surely, this is why God has sent the great shaking of which he has been warning us for the past 40 years.

False Teaching in the Church

I remember John Wimber's first visit to Britain in the early 1980s. He came with a message of truth – straight from the throne room of God. He said, Jesus is saying, "Give me back my church!" It was exactly the word that I was hearing and many other trusted friends who were seeing the moral and spiritual imperfections in our church structures, and the level of unbelief in high circles.

Since the publication of *Honest to God* by John Robinson, Bishop of Stepney, in 1963 we had seen the rise of unbelief among senior clergy in the Church of England and in the denominational churches. It was not just liberal scholarship that was disturbing the clergy. We had had liberal scholarship since the days of the Enlightenment, and 'Higher Criticism' had been with us since the late 19th century, but it had been taught in the context of a genuine search for truth in the biblical scrolls that had been handed down through the centuries.

The spirit of the age in the 1960s changed all that into an aggressive, destructive scrutiny of Scripture that led, not to increased knowledge of truth, but to unbelief. Archbishop Donald Coggan, following his famous broadcast to the nation in 1975 calling the nation back to faith in God, experienced unrelenting opposition from the liberal bishops who hated evangelism and openly criticised him. I too suffered from them as I have described elsewhere.[20] This revealed the destructive spirit of unbelief that was spreading from the theological colleges into the clergy and had reached levels of leadership that were now corrupting the institutions of the church.

Donald Coggan recognised this destructive spirit when he addressed the Lambeth Conference on 23 July 1978. He said,

"Some of you have given up believing that God still speaks to the church. God forgive us! We would not admit it; it would shock our congregations if we did. But we have stopped listening to God and our spiritual life has died on us, though we keep up the appearances and go through the motions."[21]

What Donald Coggan recognised was that there was death in the pot, like Elisha discovered: *"O man of God there is death in the pot!"* (2 Kings 4:40). This is what unbelief has done to the churches – the pots have become corrupted by the stew that has been poured into them from unbelieving theologians in the theological colleges!

I was ordained in 1952 and before that I had four years in theological college, and I have seen at first hand the spiritual corruption pouring into the church. It has been a heart-breaking experience, as it was for Donald Coggan when he was prevented from taking the gospel to the nation.

Donald Coggan was replaced by Robert Runcie, probably the most liberal Archbishop of the 20th century. Within hours of the consecration of the notorious David Jenkins as Bishop of Durham, he fiercely denied that the lightning strike upon York Minster was an act of God. When Runcie said in a BBC news broadcast that God is not in charge of the weather, this was a classic denial of the biblical concept of the Sovereignty of God.

Of course, there are plenty of ways in which the corruption of the world gets into the church through the lives of individuals, but in spiritual terms there are two major sources of unbelief entering the church. They are:

- False Prophecy
- False Teaching

---

20 *The Reshaping of Britain: Church and State since the 1960s – A Personal Reflection,* Wilberforce Publications, London, 2018, chapter one.

21 *Ibid.,* page 32.

The two are usually closely aligned and interwoven, but false prophecy is probably the more dangerous because it has strong appeal to the emotions whereas false teaching appeals more to the intellect. We will look briefly at each of these, beginning with prophecy.

False Prophecy

The Charismatic Movement was in full swing in the 1980s and there were increasing reports of things happening that were not in accordance with biblical teaching in the use of the spiritual gifts. Many people welcomed John Wimber's visit in 1984 and he became firm friends with David Watson of York with whom I sometimes shared a platform and I greatly appreciated his ministry and friendship. David was highly honoured in the Anglican Church, particularly in charismatic and evangelical sectors. So his friendship with John Wimber opened a way into church circles, not only in the Church of England, but in all the denominations where the Charismatic Movement was having an impact.

It was not long, however, before John became involved with Paul Cain who had been a disciple of the false prophet William Branham, and had been heavily involved in the Latter Rain Movement that had been widely recognised by Bible believing Christians as a heresy. Paul Cain's influence brought John into an involvement with the Kansas City Fellowship. He accepted their false prophecies which were based upon teaching that had no sound biblical basis. They believed that we were in the last generation before the second coming of Christ and that in preparation for the coming of the kingdom, God was raising up apostles with greater power than the original disciples of Jesus.

All this was based upon their false prophecies that had no basis in Scripture. These Latter-Day 'apostles' would exercise supernatural power, not only healing the sick and raising the dead, but also overcoming all opposition to the Gospel and gaining governing power in the nations. They believed that when they had subdued the nations, Jesus would return, and they would present the kingdom to him.

John Wimber was declared to be the Senior Apostle who would eventually present the kingdom to Jesus on his return. Prophecies given by these men became increasingly wild. Paul Cain was highly popular with the crowd when he gave exciting messages of the supernatural power which would transform their lives. Just months before John Wimber brought the team to London in July 1990 for two weeks of ministry in the West End of London at Holy Trinity Brompton, Paul Cain gave the following 'prophecy' in John Wimber's church in Anaheim California. I have video of him speaking with a background of great enthusiasm, cheering and clapping:

"God is saying, 'Arise and shine, for your light is come, behold the darkness will cover the earth and deep darkness, but the Lord will raise you up, the Lord will arise upon you and the nations will come to your light. You're going to Shine, Shine, Shine! You're going to be the light of day and the light of life . . . God is going to have a whole company of people that are going to be like that, and then the world will see the light and they are going to come to it, they are going to see it, all nations will come to your light and that's the way we are going to get world evangelisation.'"[22]

This kind of wild prophecy was readily absorbed by many people including senior church leaders which shows the level of deception and biblical ignorance in the church at that time. This 'prophecy', based upon Isaiah 60, promises that the public will come to "*your* light" and "*you* are going to Shine!" One of the classic marks of false prophecy is that it elevates human beings and fails to give glory to God.

When Bishop David Pytches published a book "*Some Said It Thundered*" about the exploits of the so-called Kansas City prophets in May 1990 it sold out within weeks. People flocked to hear this new level of 'prophetic revelation' said to be coming from these remarkable men. Of course, we now know that it was all nonsense because their prophecies of a great revival breaking out in October 1990 proved to be false, and several of the so-called 'prophets' were subsequently exposed for sins of the flesh. But at that time many senior church leaders, from Anglicans to Pentecostals put their faith in these men believing their words, not just in Britain, but right across the Western nations from the USA to Australia and New Zealand.

I felt very much alone at that time because of the public stand that I took in declaring that all these prophecies were nonsense. I am not saying that I was the only one to take such a stand, but I was probably the most prominent as I was the editor of the magazine *Prophecy Today* which in 1990 had the largest circulation of any Christian

22 Quoted in *Blessing the Church*, pages 133-134.

magazine in Britain. In the July 1990 edition of the magazine I wrote a three page demolition of the book *'Some Said It Thundered'* and gave my own detailed investigation of the Kansas City Fellowship whom I had visited and studied their teaching, which I said was "more like the powers of magicians and witch doctors than a prophet of God".[23]

Our sales of the magazine dropped catastrophically when John Wimber declared me to be anathema quoting Titus 3:10 against me as *"a divisive person"*. I have a drawer full of critical letters from church leaders pouring out their wrath upon me in varying degrees of intensity. It was a difficult time. But John himself repented publicly some four years later severing all connection with the Kansas City Fellowship and others linked with their teaching. John and I were reconciled shortly before his death which showed the true love and humility in his nature and it certainly was a joy for me.

False Teaching

The exposure of the Kansas City prophets did not end the matter of false prophecy in the churches. It is amazing how pernicious prophecy is in its grip upon those who are deceived by it. In dealing with false prophecy you have to demonstrate that its basis in theology and biblical teaching is unsustainable. But even when this is done those who are deceived continue to expect that their hopes will be fulfilled. So they remain vulnerable and open to the next wave of deception that comes along.

Following the spectacular failure of the much heralded revival that was supposed to start in the Excel Centre, East London in October 1990, there was no public admission of the deception by church leaders or apology to those who had paid to attend the meetings.

The leaders who publicly endorsed the false teaching and false prophecies of the Kansas City prophets in July 1990 have kept very quiet. A list of names of church leaders appeared in the Church of England Newspaper and *'Renewal'* magazine saying that they had examined the teaching of the Kansas City Fellowship which they accepted, and they commended them to the British public, endorsing them as godly men.

As far as I'm aware none of these leaders has ever publicly admitted that they were deceived or apologised to the many thousands

---

23 *Prophecy Today*, volume 6, number 4, July 1990, page 6.

of Christians who went to their meetings – especially the big meetings in the Excel Centre in London in October 1990. I'm not going to repeat their names. We each of us have to give account for our ministries to the Lord one day. But the thing that deeply troubles me is that all this false teaching got into the church and has never been torn out. It is part of the deception that has been in the church for the past 50 years and more and some of it is still being taught in churches today.

The waters were further muddied in 1994 with the coming of the next wave of deception that entered the church through the 'Toronto Blessing'. Remnants of this still hang around in many churches today. Its Latter Rain teachings are embedded in the NAR practices today that are quite widespread among churches and appear in many popular worship songs.

The Church Today

It is my belief that the Charismatic Movement that arose in the 1960s and reached its height in the 1990s, began as a genuine move of God aimed at arming the church for the battles to come from the secular forces invading the Western nations. God was equipping his people for difficult times; but far from allowing the Spirit of God to rearm, and renew the faith of his church, many churches seized the gifts for their own enjoyment, embracing false prophecy and false teaching which distorted a work of God and missed the opportunity of those days. They failed to recognise that the spiritual gifts are given to equip the church to fulfil the Great Commission! They are not given to enhance the reputation of individuals and to entertain the masses!

My purpose in briefly recounting these aberrations that got into churches of all different denominations is because they are a symbol of the lack of sound biblical study and teaching in so many churches today where leaders are more motivated by pragmatic considerations than biblical truth. Today, when God is clearly at work, shaking the nations and shaking the institutional structures of the church, he is undoubtedly warning us of severe testing yet to come. The church must be cleansed of false teaching and deception if it is to be used by God to convey his truth to the nation in these days of crisis. This is a major reason why God allowed the churches to be closed for the first time in history.

Malachi

I am indebted to my colleague David Noakes for pointing out the relevance of a word in Malachi: *"Oh, that one of you would shut the temple doors, so that you would not light useless fires on my altar!"* (Mal 1:10). That statement in Malachi is followed by the pronouncement, *"I am not pleased with you, says the Lord Almighty, and I will accept no offering from your hands."* The context of this complaint is that the priests were putting defiled offerings on the altar. The complaint was not against the ordinary people, it was against the priests, the temple authorities and their contemptible practices.

It is amazing how quickly corruption can enter an institution. Most scholars date the prophecy of Malachi around 460 BC which was only 60 years after the temple was rebuilt following the return of the people from exile in Babylon. They returned with such high hopes with the commission of Isaiah 56 to rebuild the temple as *a "house of prayer for all nations"* and the objectives set out in Isaiah 49, for the people of Israel to be a *"light for the Gentiles"* and take the message of God's salvation to all nations. But within a short space of time the priests were up to their old practices of offering defiled sacrifices which made the worship of the temple unacceptable to God.

God's intention for the exile in Babylon was to produce a redeemed remnant, purified from idolatry and committed to the missionary task of taking his truth to all nations. This mission was emphasised in the next verse in Malachi: *"My name will be great among the nations, from the rising to the setting of the sun. In every place incense and pure offerings will be brought to my name, because my name will be great among the nations, says the Lord Almighty"* (Mal 1:11).

That mission for taking the word of God to all nations was not fulfilled until some 400 years later on the Day of Pentecost when people from many nations heard the testimony of the Apostles who were eyewitnesses of the Risen Christ and some 3,000 became believers on that day. God's intention for his message of salvation to be taken to all nations began to be fulfilled that day. But the temple authorities, the state religion, soon began to harass the Apostles and to oppose their message.

It was not long before Stephen was stoned to death for daring to say to the leaders: *"You stiff-necked people, with uncircumcised hearts and ears! You are just like your fathers: you always resist the Holy Spirit! Was there ever a prophet your fathers did not persecute?"* (Acts 7:51-52). We next read that *"On that day a great persecution broke out against the church at Jerusalem".* But as the new believers were driven out of the City, they took with them the gospel and worldwide evangelism began.

The Church Today

If we jump 2000 years to today and ask why the churches were closed, we have to conclude that God was fulfilling his declared purpose of shaking everything including the institutional churches. And this is where it is necessary to distinguish between the true 'ecclesia' as 'communities of believers' and the institutions that are called 'churches'. It is surely the institutions that are being shaken. The faith of the true believers could not be shaken by the closure of buildings.

Many innovative ways of supporting local congregations of believers were discovered during the lockdown. The use of different kinds of media on the Internet resulted in gospel messages being heard by many people who would not normally go to a church building and this provided lessons for church leaders seeking to find ways of reaching beyond their usual congregation. But how much has been learned that will be valuable for reaching people with the truth in the future? Will church leaders simply go back to the old ways of doing things that have seen a steady decline in most church congregations over the past 50 years?

It is yet to be seen whether leaders of the denominational churches have truly learned anything from the lockdown period. We know that when God issues a command to shake everything, he intends it to be effective. In Amos 9:9 he says: *"I will give the command, and I will shake the house of Israel among all the nations as grain is shaken in a sieve, and not a pebble will reach the ground."* God's intention at that time was to separate the good grain from everything else that could contaminate it. This was surely his intention in closing the churches; to use the shock of the closure to take away the traditional human props from every believer and make them seek the Lord and him alone as the basis of their faith.

For church leaders the purpose was to give the opportunity for re-examining the mission of the church and to reflect upon the worldly values that have gained a stronghold in the institutions and in the lives of many individuals. The Roman Catholic church is more like a global business corporation. It can hardly be compared with the little communities of believers, the 'ecclesia' of the New Testament.

Global Institutions

Was it ever God's intention for us to create these monster institutions that we call churches? The Church of England, the Methodist Church, the Church of Scotland, the Church In Wales and other denominations follow the principles of parliamentary democracy in their decision-making procedures, passing resolutions and taking votes instead of spreading issues before the Lord, spending time in fervent intercession and waiting until they could all say *"It seems good to the Holy Spirit and to us"*, as they did at the Council of Jerusalem (Acts 15). That is theocracy – not democracy!

The structures of the churches have become so dominated by democratic procedures that we do not even realise the extent to which they have drifted away from the word of God and his intention for his people. We have already referred to Archbishop Donald Coggan's statement to the Anglican Church's governing body, the Lambeth Conference, that many of its leaders had ceased to listen to God. This could be said of leaders in all the churches and denominations where the structures rather than the mission now dominate the institutions.

I have seen this at first hand and, like Jeremiah, I have wept because I know the urgency of the message that the church should be declaring to the world. The message is being stifled by the ungodly structures of the church. I was a friend and close adviser to Archbishop Rowan Williams who constantly came up against what I used to call "the Lambeth Mafia" that controlled the institution. (Rowan always gently refuted this!)

Right at the start of his time in Lambeth Palace, Rowan hit a wall of opposition. He wanted to bring with him as his personal chaplain the man who had served him well when he was Archbishop of Wales and with whom he had a close spiritual relationship. But the Lambeth Mafia utterly refused to countenance such a thing and he was forced to have a chaplain of their choice. This set the pattern for his 10 years of institutional service in which the godly counsel he could have given was too often frustrated.

Powers of Darkness

I used to feel the presence of a spirit of heaviness as soon as I walked into Lambeth Palace. This was nothing new: it was there when I used to visit Dr George Carey in the 1990s and even back in the 1970s when Donald Coggan was Archbishop. It is not connected with the resident, but it is part of the system that controls the institution.

I shared this with a friend, the Rev Geoff Waggett, a Church in Wales priest whom I have known for many years. He also had a personal friendship with Rowan and on several occasions, he stayed in Lambeth Palace where he had exactly the same experience of the presence of powers of darkness. On one occasion when Geoff was staying there, Dr Sentamu the Archbishop of York was also there with Rowan, and Geoff gave them a prophetic word. He told Rowan about his experience and later Geoff and Rowan together went around the building praying in each room against those powers of ungodly control.

Unbelief

But, of course, the problems within the Church of England run much deeper and are rooted in unbelief. It is the same problem that Jesus confronted when he quoted the words of Isaiah *"Though seeing, they do not see; though hearing they do not hear or understand"* (Matt 13:13).

The words originally given to Isaiah were a devastating command – *"Go and tell this people: be ever hearing but never understanding; be ever seeing but never perceiving"* (Is 6:9). In the Hebrew this is an imperative, but in the Septuagint version of the Bible it was translated as a simple present tense. As we have noted, Jesus did not quote from the Hebrew: he quoted from the Greek text; probably because he recognised the simple fact that the leaders of the institutional religion of Israel would never understand – that there was a blockage in their spiritual life that prevented them from ever understanding – *"They will be ever seeing, but never perceiving"*. This is exactly the same situation that we have in the institutional state religion in Britain and it is replicated in the Roman Catholic Church and in the Protestant denominations.

The situation is rightly described by Jesus in his encounter with Nicodemus who was searching for the truth, but he was so under the dominance of the temple religious institution that he came by night secretly; but he simply could not understand when Jesus told him that he had to be born again. Jesus summarised the problem *"This is the verdict: light has come into the world, but men loved darkness instead of light because their deeds were evil"* (John 3:19).

Light and Darkness

The whole Gospel of John is about light coming into the world which he describes as the advent of the Logos in his prologue. But light and darkness are not two separate zones – the whole purpose of light is to overcome the darkness, to dispel it completely. But when we light a lamp in a room it inevitably casts shadows although its purpose is to fill the room with light. Unless the room is completely empty there will be shadows. The clash between light and darkness is inevitable because **the light has come, not just to *expose* the darkness, but to *banish* it for ever.**

That is the nature of the battle that is raging in the world today between the forces of darkness and the light. The darkness hates the light because they know they will be extinguished in the end. But that same battle is being fought in the church where the forces of darkness have gained a stronghold.

Breaking the Barrier of Unbelief

The only thing that can break the barrier of unbelief is a new mindset. But this requires the death of the old mind and the birth of the new mind. This is what Jesus meant when he told Nicodemus that he had to be born again. And this is what Paul meant when he said: *"If anyone is in Christ, there is a new creation, the old has gone, the new has come!"* (2 Cor 5:17). That certainly was my experience. It changed my life and remoulded the ministry that I exercised. It is something I try to share with fellow ministers and clergy who have had a similar training to my own.

I speak from experience, having gone through the academic mill of liberal theology from undergraduate to doctorate. I know what it is to allow the seed to fall into the ground and die before new life can be born. It was not easy, after years of academic study to allow it all to drop into the ground and die so that faith could be reborn, and then could come a fresh approach to the Bible with a mind re-energised by faith that enabled a new creation to be born with an eagerness to re-explore the word of God and make new discoveries, like the man in Jesus's parable who found treasure buried in his field.

Ezekiel describes this as a promise from God "*I will cleanse you of all your impurities and from all your idols. I will give you a new heart and put a new Spirit in you; I will remove from you your heart of stone and give you a heart of flesh. And I will put my Spirit in you and move you to follow my decrees and be careful to keep my laws*" (Ezek 36:25-27). But will this be the outcome of the crisis upon the churches of Britain? Surely that is God's intention of ensuring that the great shaking of the nation reaches right into the churches.

The Future

It is far too early to assess the effects of the lockdown of church buildings and the subsequent days of hardship upon the leadership of the churches. It is my expectation that the intense economic outcome of the pandemic will severely shake the organisational structures of the churches. But I also expect to see the days become darker and more testing for Christians as the cultural Marxist bandwagon rolls on.

As that bandwagon gains in confidence, intolerance will grow against any opposition to its declared purposes of destroying the traditional marriage-based family that the LGBT movement sees as the "root of their oppression". Their hatred of committed Christians will increase, which will be all part of the rise of the Antichrist that we may expect in the last days, in the run-up to the second coming of Jesus. I foresee the possibility of legislation tightening the grip and extending the powers of the so-called 'hate laws' to include the Bible as offensive literature, and parts may be banned from being quoted in public. It may mean that the Bible-believing remnant of the true ecclesia may have to go underground in some way, in at least part of its work and witness and develop a network of support for local prayer groups scattered across the country.

A New Move of God

But I do not expect believers to be tested beyond their capacity. In fact, I believe there will be a spontaneous backlash against the increasing activity of the secular humanists as parents become more aware of the effect upon their children of the teaching they are receiving in schools that results in behavioural problems generated by increased gender uncertainty and a range of mental health problems. There is likely to be an increasing recognition that something is basically wrong in the nation. This will be reflected in the rising crime and drugs problems among young people generated by increasing unemployment.

But public disquiet will increase due to the wide range of problems in society for which there seems to be no answer in government policy. There will come a point which intercessors and watchman who are listening to the Lord will recognise, when increasing numbers of unbelievers will be raising their voices in dismay at what is happening in the nation. It is likely that life will become increasingly difficult for Christians, but this will be God shaking the nation and causing people to recognise the inability of their leaders to solve the problems the people are facing. These two social processes will go alongside each other in parallel – increased persecution of believers and increased fear and disruption in society. But believers should not fear because this will be God at work preparing the ground for a move of God.

Declaring the Word of God

This will be the time for the church – or at least the Bible-believing remnant in the nation – to have the courage to stand up and tell the Government and the people why judgment has come upon the land: because we have defied the God of creation by murdering multitudes of babies, defiling the land with the blood of the innocent. We have defied the truth about marriage and gender and dared to teach vile lies to our children. We have despised our Judaeo-Christian heritage, allowing other religions to establish spiritual strongholds in the land. We have made only half-hearted attempts to stamp out anti-Semitism and allowed a whole generation of young people to become increasingly intolerant. They are driven by destructive values and teachings, fed by the forces of darkness, that have been able to take root because their generation has no knowledge of biblical truth.

We must declare that there will be no remission in the shaking of the nation until there is repentance and change. If there is no change, we will go on struggling with all the problems and fears in society today, wondering if normal times will ever return. Undoubtedly, once Christians begin declaring the truth in the public square it will increase persecution upon them. But this is all part of the purposes of God. The blood of the martyrs has always been the seed of the church since the days of Tertullian. But the believers will have to remain closely listening to the Lord for his direction, because judgment always must be declared in the context of God's loving good purposes for the human beings whom he loves. This underlines the need for believers to know how to 'stand in the Council of the Lord', to listen to him attentively, and to be obedient in everything that he says.

Learning to Grieve

I believe the Lord wants his people to grieve over the state of the nation. We cannot effectively call for repentance unless we ourselves have a true spirit of repentance which is rooted in grief. We need to recognise the extent to which the churches in Britain are responsible for the state of the nation. We have a whole generation of young people who have no plumbline of truth by which to judge right and wrong. They are the parents of the next generation who will be raising their children in a godless society with no knowledge of the God who created them and who longs for them to be in a right relationship with him.

I believe the older generation of which I am a part, before we go to glory, should learn to grieve for our share of responsibility for the state of the nation. We need to learn to lament as the people of Jerusalem did after its destruction in 586 BC. I cannot read the book of Lamentations without tears in my eyes. "*The roads to Zion mourn, for no one comes to her appointed feasts. All her gateways are desolate, her priests groan, her maidens grieve, and she is in bitter anguish. Her foes have become her masters; her enemies are at ease. The Lord has brought her grief because of her many sins*" (Lam 1:4-5).

But surely, we should be grieving for the millions going to a lost eternity in our own nation. When I began my ministry in the 1950s the churches were full. I'm not saying we were a godly nation – far from it, but everyone had some knowledge of the Bible and the truth between right and wrong so that they could be accountable to God for their own lives and those of their children. Today we have a whole generation who have never had any access to biblical teaching either at home or in school. It is the older generation who have allowed this tragedy to happen through its 'Silent Churches' – struck dumb by unbelief – who have absorbed that culture of the day rather than declare the word of the living God. Yes, we need to learn to lament and grieve before God before we go to glory, because God always responds to the tears of his people. In the heart of the book of Lamentations there is the most beautiful word of faith and hope. In the midst of all its grief there come these beautiful words:

"Yet this I called to mind and therefore I have hope: because of the Lord's great love we are not consumed, for his compassions never fail. They are new every morning; great is your faithfulness. I say to myself, "The Lord is my portion; therefore I will wait for him." The Lord is good to those whose hope is in him, to the one who seeks him; it is good to wait quietly for the salvation of the Lord" (Lam 3:21-26).

God's Response

I believe that when the people of God, the faithful remnant in Britain, learn to grieve there will indeed be a response from God. When we truly recognise the awfulness of the godless state of our nation and how we have broken every one of the commandments of our God – our tears of lament will bring an immediate response from our Father in Heaven as the father in the parable of Jesus hurried to his penitent son. This is a lesson we can learn from the vision given to the prophet Ezekiel that we know as the 'Valley of the Dry Bones' in Ezekiel 37.

The Prophet was not just taken in the Spirit to see a valley covered with the bones of his countrymen, but he was *"taken to and fro among them"*. He was forced to see the full reality of the dry bones in the valley of death that was the consequence of God removing his cover of protection from over the nation. He had to recognise the full horror of the consequences of the sinfulness of the people and the justice of God before the good news could come. This is what we have to do today and why we need to lament.

The Dry Bones

Then God promised an outpouring of his Spirit to bring new life to his people. *"Can these bones live?"* This was followed by the command: ***"Prophesy to these bones and say to them, dry bones, hear the word of the Lord!"*** – (How we long to hear that command in our nation today! Will the silent church regain the power to declare the word of the Lord while there is yet time?)

Immediately after this came the promise *"I will make breath enter you, and you will come to life."* Our English translations say that there was *"a rattling sound"* as the bones came together. This is a terrible translation! The Hebrew literally says ***"there was a thunderous noise"*** as the bones came together. This vision represents a colossal miracle taking place as the power of God swept over the mountains descending into the valley of death, bringing new life into the dry skeletons. Only the English could be so polite (or pathetic) as to call it *"a rattling sound"*.

The Thunderous Noise

I believe this vision of new life coming into the dry bones has great relevance for us today. The thunderous noise will be heard in Britain when the faithful remnant come grieving before the Lord, and with utter disregard of self-preservation they will declare the truth to the godless generation at the helm of the nation. The heavens will open to pour new life upon those who respond to the word of God.

Back in the 1980s when we first heard the warning of a great shaking, we also heard that it would become so intense that even unbelievers would be crying out to God for help – saying **"Oh God help us!"** At that point there would be a new openness to truth and a great opportunity for believers to declare the gospel, resulting in multitudes accepting Jesus as Lord and Saviour.

We may not be far off that day when *'the thunderous noise'* will once again be heard, when the Spirit of God descends upon the faithful remnant – breaking the silence of the church! And re-energising and equipping God's people with the boldness to declare the word of God to the nation – and multitudes will hear the truth and accept Jesus as their Lord and Saviour!!

"After this I heard what sounded like the roar of a great multitude in heaven shouting: Hallelujah! Salvation and glory and power belong to our God, for true and just are his judgments" (Rev 19:1).